The Life and Resurrection of Jesus Christ:
A Biblical Narrative

An In-Depth Exploration Through
the King James Bible

Gary E. Risenhoover

Published by Kinetic Digital Publishers

www.kineticdigitalpublishers.com

For permissions, inquiries, or other correspondence, please visit our website.

LCCN: 2026906005

ISBN eBook: 979-8-90235-093-4

ISBN Paperback: 979-8-90235-094-1

ISBN Hardcover: 979-8-90235-095-8

TABLE OF CONTENTS

Prophecies and the Coming Light...3

A Silent Night in Bethlehem 18

The Baptism and the Holy Dove 30

Teaching on the Mount..43

Miracles of Light and Hope..58

Friendships and Fables..77

The Journey to Jerusalem: Shadows Ascend 94

The Last Supper's Sacred Feast.....................................108

The Agony in Gethsemane 121

The Passion: A Passionate Portrait................................134

The Silence of the Tomb 146

Resurrection Dawn: Light Unbound 159

Thank You, Bold Explorer! 172

Hey There, Amazing Reader!

Welcome to this thrilling journey through the pages you've just picked up! This book wasn't born overnight; it's the product of countless hours of brainstorming, late-night research, and a relentless passion to uncover stories that matter. I wanted to create something that grabs your attention from the first word and never lets go. Every chapter is a bridge connecting curiosity with discovery, designed to ignite your imagination and challenge your perspectives.

Crafting this book involved diving deep into a sea of information, cross-examining every fact, anecdote, and insight. I sought out voices that are often unheard and perspectives that shake up the norm. This isn't just a collection of facts, it's an invitation to think, question, and explore. Through these pages, you will encounter fascinating ideas and inspiring tales that align with the pulse of today's world, yet reach out to timeless truths.

Bringing this work to life demanded collaboration and feedback from a vibrant community of thinkers, dreamers, and doers. Their perspectives sharpened the narrative and fueled the energy you'll feel in every sentence. It's a reflection of many minds and hearts committed to making this experience unforgettable.

As you embark on this literary voyage, I encourage you to dive in with an open mind and an eager spirit. Challenge the ideas, savor the stories, and let your own imagination run wild. This book waits to be your launchpad into new realms of thought and feeling.

Whether you're here for inspiration, knowledge, or just a captivating read, you're in the right place. Prepare yourself for a rollercoaster of emotions and insights that will surprise you, provoke you, and maybe even transform you. The world inside these covers is lively, vibrant, and ready to welcome you.

Remember, the true magic of a book lies not only in the words but in how they spark something inside of you. So, turn the page with excitement. What's coming next might just change the way you see everything.

Thank you for choosing this adventure. Let's make these pages come alive together.

Here's to epic journeys ahead!

Gary E. Risenhoover

Prophecies and the Coming Light

Voices of the Ancient Prophets

Long before the dawn of the New Testament era, long before the bustling towns of Galilee echoed with the footsteps of a carpenter's son, the ancient prophets arose as voices in the wilderness, urgent, piercing, and inexorable. Their words, etched into the enduring scrolls of Israel's sacred history, carried the weight of divine revelation and the fervent hope of a nation longing for redemption. To enter into the world of these prophets is to step into a landscape marked by turmoil and promise, shadows and light, exile and restoration, a world in which the promise of the Messiah shimmered like a distant star, guiding all who would listen toward a greater salvation.

Among these prophets, Isaiah, Micah, and Jeremiah stand as towering figures whose proclamations shape the very foundation of Messianic expectation. Their oracles, often poetic and vivid, thread through the fabric of Israel's collective memory with a clarity and power that transcend time. These were not mere predictions; they were living words, spoken by men deeply attuned to the voice of God, uttered in moments of national crisis and spiritual renewal. To hear them anew is to understand that the coming light, the Messiah, was not a sudden event but the culmination of centuries of divine dialogue between heaven and earth.

Isaiah's prophetic vision unfolds with astonishing grandeur. Living in the turbulent 8th century BCE, he witnessed the threats of Assyrian conquest and the fracturing of the Israelite kingdom. Yet amid these dangers, Isaiah's voice resounds with a message deeply infused with hope and redemption. "For unto us a child is born, unto us a son is given: and the government shall be upon his shoulder" (Isaiah 9:6). These words, pregnant with promise, speak of a ruler who transcends earthly crowns, a child whose kingdom endures forever, a bearer of peace and justice. The majesty of Isaiah's metaphor paints a majestic portrait, depicting the Messiah as "Wonderful, Counselor, The mighty God, The everlasting Father, The Prince of Peace." In these titles lie not only royal authority but divine essence, conferring upon the coming Savior a unique identity that bridges the human and the divine.

Isaiah's prophecies do not stop at royal exaltation. He portrays the suffering servant, a figure bearing the sins and sorrows of many. This servant, marred and afflicted, becomes the vessel of atonement and healing, a pattern later echoed in the life and passion of Jesus Christ. "He was wounded for our transgressions, he was bruised for our iniquities" (Isaiah 53:5). The pathos of these words conveys a profound spiritual truth: redemption will come through suffering and sacrifice. Isaiah's vision thus encompasses the full spectrum of the Messiah's mission, from joyous birth and righteous reign to sacrificial death and victorious resurrection.

Parallel to Isaiah's majestic visions is the voice of Micah, a prophet whose words are both poetic and piercing in their simplicity. Active during the 8th century BCE as well, Micah's message was directed toward the social injustices and moral failures of his time. Yet beyond his call to repentance lies a luminous promise of hope. It is Micah who foretells the humble origins of the coming ruler: "But thou, Bethlehem Ephratah, though thou be little among the thousands of Judah, yet out of thee shall he come forth unto me that is to be ruler in Israel" (Micah 5:2). This declaration anchors the Messiah not in grandeur but in a small, unassuming town, foreshadowing the humility and earthly roots of Christ's birth. The power of this prophecy lies in its insistence that greatness will emerge from seeming insignificance, that the eternal King will come clothed in simplicity and approachability.

Micah's prophecy also stretches forward to envision a future era of peace, when nations will "beat their swords into plowshares, and their spears into pruning hooks" (Micah 4:3). This vision invites readers to grasp the Messianic age not only as a historical event but as a transformative epoch, one that promises the end of conflict and the dawn of universal harmony. Embedded here is an ethical summons, a call for believers to anticipate and to partake in the reconciliation and restoration heralded by the Messiah.

Jeremiah's voice, rising in the early 7th century BCE, carries a different tone, deeply marked by heartbreak and hope amid exile. Known as the "weeping prophet," Jeremiah bore witness to the destruction of Jerusalem and the devastation of the temple, yet his prophecies also unveil the steadfast faithfulness of God in the midst of judgment. Among his most poignant promises is the assurance of a new covenant: "Behold, the days come, saith the LORD, that I will make a new covenant with the house of Israel, and with the house of Judah" (Jeremiah 31:31). This covenant, different from the Mosaic law written on stone, would be inscribed upon hearts, a divine transformation that prefigures the inner renewal brought by Christ.

Jeremiah's oracles resonate with themes of restoration and divine intimacy. He speaks of a time when God's people will no longer be cast away or shamed but will live securely, loved and protected. "They shall teach no more every man his neighbor, and every man his brother, saying, Know the LORD: for they shall all know me, from the least of them unto the greatest of them" (Jeremiah 31:34). Here lies the promise of universal knowledge of God, a consummation of the Messianic mission that extends beyond political deliverance to embrace spiritual enlightenment and reconciliation.

To fully appreciate these prophetic voices, one must consider the historical and cultural context in which they arose. The Israelite nation stood at the crossroads of ancient empires, caught between Egyptian decline, Assyrian aggression, Babylonian upheaval, and later Persian dominance. Political instability and social turmoil often accompanied spiritual infidelity and moral compromise. Prophets were not merely seers but covenant enforcers, challenging kings and people alike to return to God's standards and to place their trust in His promises. Their words often met resistance and ridicule, yet their faithfulness carved a lasting imprint on Israel's collective soul.

The Messianic prophecies, then, are not isolated statements but integral to God's unfolding redemptive plan. They weave through Israel's story as a living thread, connecting the shadowed past to a luminous future. Each voice complements and enriches the others, creating a multifaceted portrait of hope that embraces both triumph and suffering, judgment and mercy, exile and restoration.

The poetic cadence of Isaiah's visions, the earthy realism of Micah's promises, and the heartfelt lamentation and hope of Jeremiah together form a symphony of expectation. This symphony anticipates a Messiah who would embody divine justice and mercy, who would reign in peace and sacrifice Himself for the sins of many, and who would establish an eternal covenant written on the human heart. Each word spoken by these prophets is fueled not by mere speculation but by the breath of God Himself, carrying the certainty of fulfillment across the centuries.

Moreover, the enduring power of these prophecies lies in their ongoing relevance. For the faithful, they remain a source of spiritual sustenance, reminders that God's promises transcend historical contingencies and personal circumstances. The Messianic hope they enkindle invites believers to live in faithful expectation and joyful assurance, knowing that the dawn has come and yet still gathers in fullness.

Thus, the ancient prophets stand as beacons, their voices echoing through time to illuminate the path toward Christ. They invite us to listen deeply, to hear beyond the literal and into the spiritual heart of their words. In their proclamations, we glimpse not only the future Messiah but also the character of God, a God who is just and merciful, patient and faithful, eternally committed to the salvation of His people.

As we meditate on these prophetic voices, we come to see prophecy as more than prediction; it is a divine invitation to participation. The prophets call us to align ourselves with God's redemptive purpose, to live as those who await the coming light not passively but actively, shining forth righteousness, peace, and hope in a world still marked by darkness. In this way, the threads of ancient prophecy are woven into the fabric of our own faith journey, connecting the past, present, and future in an unbroken story of salvation.

In the final reckoning, the words of Isaiah, Micah, and Jeremiah are living oracles, words that shaped history and continue to shape hearts. They stand as eternal testimony to God's unchanging plan: to send forth a Messiah, the Son of God, who would bring light to the nations, heal the broken, and restore the covenant of grace. This profound legacy of prophecy, rich with poetic beauty and divine truth, beckons all who read it to stand in awe before the unfolding mystery of redemption and to renew their hope in the coming light that has indeed dawned in Jesus Christ.

Heaven's Promise: The Messianic Hope

From the earliest days of Israel's history, the promise of a coming deliverer was woven into the tapestry of divine revelation, a luminous thread of hope that flickered through the shadows of exile, suffering, and longing. This hope, borne on the wings of prophetic utterances, carried the weight of heaven's own anticipation: the promise of a Messiah, an anointed one who would bring restoration not only to a people but to all creation. As we turn our gaze toward the sacred texts, we encounter a celestial panorama where the yearning of the Hebrew heart was mapped out in signs and shadows, ultimately fulfilled in the person of Jesus Christ.

The Messianic hope was no vague wish or distant fantasy; it was grounded upon God's faithful declarations, made through prophets whose voices bore the certainty of divine inspiration. These scriptures, penned centuries before the birth of Jesus, outline unmistakable markers, the Messiah's lineage, His peculiar birth, and His destined mission. Each prophecy carries the weight of a divine promise, confirmed by the historical, spiritual, and theological reality converging in the New Testament narrative.

The very foundation of the messianic expectation begins with God's covenant with Abraham. In Genesis 12:3, God declares, "And in thee shall all families of the earth be blessed." This pronouncement establishes that from Abraham's seed would flow a blessing far beyond the confines of Israel. Later, in Genesis 22:18, the promise is reiterated: "In thy seed shall all the nations of the earth be blessed; because thou hast obeyed my voice." This seed, as the scriptures unfold, is no ordinary descendant but the one through whom salvation and divine reconciliation would come to the world.

Prophecies concerning the Messiah's lineage particularly underscore the Davidic covenant. To David, king and saint of Israel, God made a solemn promise documented in 2 Samuel 7:12–13: "When thy days be fulfilled, and thou shalt sleep with thy fathers, I will set up thy seed after thee, which shall proceed out of thy bowels, and I will establish his kingdom. He shall build a house for my name, and I will establish the throne of his kingdom forever." This royal line was to culminate in a king whose reign would never end, a perpetual ruler who would restore Israel and bring peace to the earth.

Throughout the Psalms and the prophetic writings, this eternal king is portrayed with a blend of humility, majesty, and suffering, dimensions that would find their full expression in Jesus Christ. Psalm 2, for example, depicts a divine Son who is appointed by God Himself, whose rule is both righteous and victorious. "Thou art my Son; this day have I begotten thee" (Psalm 2:7) heralds a sonship intimately linked with divine authority. Similarly, Isaiah 9:6–7 proclaims the coming of a child whose government will be upon his shoulders, naming him "Wonderful, Counselor, The mighty God, The everlasting Father, The Prince of Peace," underscoring the unparalleled nature of his kingship.

The signature of this Messianic child is also deeply embedded in the mysterious manner of His birth, a miraculous incarnation that transcends natural order, signifying the divine entering into human history. Isaiah 7:14 declares, "Therefore the Lord himself shall give you a sign; Behold, a virgin shall conceive, and bear a son, and shall call his name Immanuel." This prophetic word, uttered centuries before the arrival of Jesus, takes on startling clarity in the Gospel of Matthew 1:22–23, where Matthew testifies that Jesus' birth to the virgin Mary fulfills this ancient promise: "Behold, a virgin shall be with child, and shall bring forth a son, and they shall call his name Emmanuel, which being interpreted is, God with us."

The miraculous nature of the incarnation, where divinity clothed itself in humanity, is both a fulfillment of prophecy and a profound theological declaration. The divine promise was no mere metaphor or symbolism; it was a real manifestation of God's redemptive plan coming to life. This unique birth qualified Jesus for a mission unlike any other, and importantly, tied Him genealogically to the house of David, fulfilling the ancient expectation that the Messiah would arise from David's lineage. The genealogies recorded in Matthew 1 and Luke 3 meticulously trace Jesus' human ancestry from Abraham through David, thereby reinforcing His rightful claim to the throne promised by God.

Beyond birth and lineage, the mission of the Messiah was frequently foreshadowed by descriptions of his suffering, redemption, and kingdom. Isaiah 53 serves as a poignant description of the Suffering Servant, one who would be "despised and rejected of men; a man of sorrows, and acquainted with grief" (Isaiah 53:3). This portrait, so vivid and compelling, is echoed in the passion narratives of Jesus. The servant's silent submission to suffering, bearing the iniquities of others and being "wounded for our transgressions," ushers in the understanding of Jesus' sacrificial role, not as a conquering warrior who comes to wield earthly power but as a Redeemer whose victory is achieved through selfless suffering and death.

This theme of sacrifice was not disconnected from hope; it was a necessary pathway to a new and everlasting covenant. Jeremiah foretold of a covenant written not on tablets of stone but on hearts: "I will put my law in their inward parts, and write it in their hearts" (Jeremiah 31:33). Jesus Himself proclaimed fulfillment of this hope, inaugurating the new covenant through His life, death, and resurrection, thereby fulfilling the divine plan anticipated since time immemorial.

The eleventh chapter of the prophet Micah, though lesser-known in popular discourse, contains one of the most precise geographical prophecies related to the birthplace of the Messiah. Micah 5:2 states, "But thou, Bethlehem Ephratah, though thou be little among the thousands of Judah, yet out of thee shall he come forth unto me that is to be ruler in Israel; whose goings forth have been from of old, from everlasting." This passage clearly identifies Bethlehem, a humble and unassuming town, as the birthplace of the eternal ruler, one whose origins are from everlasting times, affirming the paradox of eternity taking form in a temporal place.

When the events surrounding Jesus' birth unfolded in Bethlehem, as reported in Luke 2, the prophetic promises found their living expression. Shepherds, under the celestial glow of angelic proclamation, bore witness to a "Savior, which is Christ the Lord" (Luke 2:11), revealing that heaven's promise had been realized on earth.

The spiritual yearning that permeated Hebrew expectation was no mere passive waiting but an ardent hope that shaped identity and destiny. The Psalms, a treasury of Israelite devotion, resonate with cries and anticipation for the coming king. Psalm 72, attributed to Solomon but messianic in its scope, prays for a righteous ruler who "shall have dominion also from sea to sea, and from the river unto the ends of the earth" (Psalm 72:8). The longing yearned not only for deliverance from physical enemies but for an era of justice, peace, and divine presence.

The New Testament writers, steeped in these scriptures, interpreted Jesus' life and mission as their fulfillment. The apostle Paul, in his letter to the Romans 1:3–4, affirms Jesus "was made of the seed of David according to the flesh; and declared to be the Son of God with power, according to the spirit of holiness, by the resurrection from the dead." This declaration unites Jesus' human descent with divine endorsement, culminating in the resurrection as God's ultimate vindication.

John's Gospel opens with a majestic theological assertion: "In the beginning was the Word, and the Word was with God, and the Word was God" (John 1:1). Here is the eternal pre-existent divine Logos, who "became flesh, and dwelt among us, (and we beheld his glory...)" (John 1:14). This incarnation, the Word made flesh, is the apex of heavenly promise fulfilled, signaling God's profound commitment to redeem and restore.

The messianic hope transcended national boundaries as it became clear that Jesus' mission encompassed all peoples. The prophet Isaiah had already envisioned this universal scope, proclaiming that the Messiah would be "a light to lighten the Gentiles, and the glory of thy people Israel" (Isaiah 49:6). Jesus' ministry echoed this calling, extending salvation beyond Israel to all nations, thus fulfilling the Abrahamic promise and affirming God's intention for universal blessing.

In reflecting on the messianic prophecies, one cannot overlook the manner in which they weave together the human and divine, the temporal and eternal, the sorrowful and triumphant. The promises are suffused with a transforming hope, casting light like starlight over a waiting earth, inviting every reader to behold the grandeur of God's plan made manifest in Jesus Christ.

To grasp the magnitude of this promise is to understand that the Messiah was never intended to be a mere political savior or an earthly king. Rather, He is the incarnate Word who bridges heaven and earth, the suffering servant who conquers death, and the eternal king whose kingdom is both present and yet to be fully realized. This dynamic interplay of prophecy and fulfillment offers readers a living narrative, not confined to the pages of history but active and stirring in the depths of the human soul.

In this sacred dialogue between God and humanity, the messianic promise energizes faith, inspires worship, and beckons believers to participate in the unfolding story of redemption. The hope that once kindled the hearts of prophets now shines vividly in the person of Jesus, inviting all to embrace the divine fulfillment that transforms darkness into light, despair into joy, and death into life eternal.

Thus, Heaven's promise stands as a radiant beacon, a celestial covenant that whispers throughout the ages: "The Messiah has come. His life is the answer. His resurrection is the victory. Come, behold the

Lamb of God who takes away the sin of the world." This profound truth, ritualized through prophecy and realized in history, remains the cornerstone of Christian hope and the foundation of everlasting faith.

The Promise Illuminated: Preparing Hearts

In the silent hush that blankets the earth before the dawn, the world stands poised in a moment of breathless expectancy. The age-old promises whispered through the lips of prophets long gone mingle now with the aching hearts of a people stirred by the winds of change. From the dry wilderness to the crowded cities of Judea, there stirs a whisper, a faint glimmer of hope, a promise about to be fulfilled. This is the time when the shadowed twilight of the Old Covenant yields to the first rays of a new and radiant dawn. It is here, in the sacred space between despair and hope, judgment and mercy, that the stage prepares itself for the coming Light, and preparing hearts become the silent heralds of salvation.

The world of Israel, gripped by centuries of anticipation, moves under the weight of a profound spiritual restlessness. Her elders remember the covenant made upon Mount Sinai, the law given by God through Moses, a law that bore the solemn character of holiness and justice. It is a law that reveals God's righteous demands upon His people, yet also lays bare their inability to fulfill them without divine compassion. The people live under the careful gaze of this covenant, the Old Testament law etched into stone, commanding both fear and reverence. But now, as the generations pass, the promises of a coming Deliverer grow more urgent, more vivid, painting the horizon of hope with colors of salvation and grace.

The prophets in their day spoke of this coming mercy, their words like sparks cast into the dark, each igniting a flame of expectancy. Isaiah, with his vision of a suffering servant who would bear the sins of many, told of a light dawning for those who sit in darkness. Jeremiah spoke tenderly of a new covenant inscribed not on tablets of stone but on hearts of flesh, a covenant that would transform and renew from within. Micah foretold the birth of a ruler in Bethlehem who would shepherd His people in peace. These ancient voices echo softly through time, reverberating in the hearts of Israel's people, enkindling a yearning for redemption that nothing else can quench.

Amidst this spiritual awakening, John the Baptist emerges as a towering figure, the chosen herald who bridges the old and the new. Clothed in camel's hair, a wild voice crying out in the wilderness, John stirs the souls of those weary and burdened under the weight of their sins. His call is one of repentance, a call to prepare: "Prepare ye the way of the Lord, make his paths straight." As he stands at the threshold of this new epoch, he embodies the very essence of preparation, a living symbol of the urgent need to ready every heart for the coming of the Messiah.

John's ministry is marked by austere holiness and piercing conviction. In the barren deserts near the Jordan River, where the wind whispers ancient secrets and the earth thirsts for rain, John's voice breaks forth like thunder. He calls out to Pharisees, Sadducees, and sinners alike, warning of impending judgment but, even more, pointing to the mercy about to be revealed in Jesus Christ. In his baptismal waters, a divine invitation is offered: to cleanse the soul, to turn away from sin, and to welcome the Kingdom of Heaven. His baptism is not mere ritual; it is the washing away of old fears and failures, the opening of hearts eager to receive the promised Light.

But John is not alone in this landscape of expectation. The collective consciousness of Israel, a tapestry woven from millennia of longing and covenantal faithfulness, beats steadily beneath the surface of daily life. Pilgrims gather at the temple, their prayers rising like incense. Mothers rock their children, telling stories of a God who remembers His promises. Elders recount the times of Abraham,

David, and the prophets, reminding all that the God who called their fathers remains faithful still. Into this rich soil, the seed of hope is planted anew.

Yet, this time is also one of unrest. The Roman occupation casts a shadow over the land, and oppression presses heavily upon the shoulders of the people. In the synagogues, tongues speak of revolt even as hearts seek peace. There is a tension between the desire for political deliverance and the deeper yearning for spiritual salvation. The people are caught between fear and hope, justice and mercy, the Old Covenant's stern demands and the promise of a new covenant of grace.

This tension shapes the spiritual atmosphere like the heavy clouds gathered before a storm that will cleanse the earth. It is a holy unrest, a stirring of the soul that cannot be silenced. The coming of Jesus is anticipated not with naive expectation, but with a profound awareness that God's justice and mercy will meet in Him. It is known, implicitly, that the salvation promised is not merely from political enemies or earthly trials, but from sin and death themselves.

Throughout this period, the imagery of light grows ever more vital. Darkness is no mere absence; it is the symbol of estrangement from God, of ignorance and despair. Into this darkness, the prophets had foretold, a light would shine, a light so radiant that it would dispel the shadows and reveal the path to eternal life. As John proclaims, "He that cometh after me is mightier than I... he shall baptize you with the Holy Ghost, and with fire." This is the Light coming to illumine every heart willing to receive it.

The metaphor of dawn, with its slow unfolding and gradual illumination, serves as a fitting emblem for this time of preparation. Just as the first rays of morning light gently sweep away the beauty of the night sky, so does this new hope begin to dissolve the weariness born of waiting and sorrow. The hearts of men and women, once hardened by years of trial and doubt, are softened by this dawning promise. The desire for salvation awakes as quietly as a prayer, deep within the soul's chamber.

In the homes of Bethlehem and the hills of Judea, in the marketplaces bustling with activity and the quiet fields where shepherds watch their flocks by night, the anticipation grows. The soil itself seems to hold its breath. Mothers whisper lullabies filled with the longing for the Messiah. Fathers recall the ancient prophecies and share them with their children, planting the seed of faith for future generations. The heartbeat of Israel quickens, and the echo of centuries of prophecy finds its crescendo in this holy expectancy.

To prepare one's heart in this time requires more than mere observance. It calls for a turning, a metanoia, that touches every corner of the spirit. It is a purification, a cleansing that mirrors the baptismal waters of Jordan, where repentance flows freely and souls emerge renewed. It is a readiness to embrace mercy wrapped in humility, and the courage to trust in God's unfolding plan despite the shadows of uncertainty.

The call of John the Baptist is thus both a spiritual summons and a poetic expression of this profound truth: the coming of Christ demands that hearts be made straight, free from the twisting entanglements of sin and fear. The winding paths of human pride and rebellion must give way to the plain road of surrender and faith. Only then can the Light be truly welcomed, the promise fully understood.

And so, as travelers who steady themselves for a pilgrimage, the people prepare to journey toward Bethlehem's star, a star whose brilliance will outshine every earthly crown and every despairing night. This star does not merely mark a place on a map; it serves as a divine beacon, guiding all who seek salvation toward the arrival of the Son of God.

In this sacred moment before the birth, the world becomes a vast and reverent temple. Every breath, every glance, every whispered prayer carries within it the weight of expectation and the hope of fulfillment. The promise illuminated by prophets, by John the Baptist, and by the yearning hearts of Israel is poised to burst forth in light and life.

To stand at this threshold is to enter into a profound mystery: that of divine love preparing to enfold a weary world. This anticipation invites the reader to join the centuries-long pilgrimage, to set their heart alongside those who awaited the dawn, and to feel the stirring within, the quiet awakening of a soul ready to receive the Light that no darkness can overcome.

As the stage is set and the lamps are trimmed, the world waits, poised between judgment and mercy, yearning and fulfillment. *The Promise Illuminated* now beckons, a call to prepare not only the paths of the land but the pathways within the heart, that when the Light appears, it may shine forth uncontested, revealing the glory of God incarnate and heralding a new beginning for all humanity.

A Silent Night in Bethlehem

The Journey to the Manger

The journey to Bethlehem was not merely a pathway etched across Jerusalem's arid landscape; it was a pilgrimage marked by profound anticipation and solemn burden. Under a sky vast and shimmering with countless stars, Mary and Joseph set forth, their steps guided by law, yet shadowed by prophecy and divine purpose. The night air was cool and sharp, a gentle chill that seeped beneath cloaks and stirred the breath into faint clouds before each inhale. The black dome above blazed with the brilliance of celestial fires, each star a witness to the unfolding covenant between heaven and earth.

Mary rode with quiet dignity astride a gentle donkey, her form wrapped in modest linens, the faint rustle of fabric meeting the night's stillness. Though weariness clung to her frame, there was in her eyes a tranquil resolve, as if the life she bore within was a light that defied the surrounding darkness. Every step the beast took upon the dusty earth stirred small clouds that caught the moon's pale silver, floating momentarily before settling again into the silence. Joseph walked beside her, his sturdy frame bent slightly forward, a staff gripped firmly in calloused hands, eyes never turning away from the narrow path ahead.

The route itself was unforgiving; a narrow, twisting way carved through hills whose rugged faces were blanched by the moonlight, their sharp edges softened by distant shadows. Occasionally, the sharp cry of a nocturnal bird echoed faintly, mingling with the rhythmic clip-clop of the donkey's hooves and the soft shuffle of Joseph's sandals against the gravel-strewn road. The air held the scent of dry earth and scattered brush, interlaced with the faintest aroma of wild thyme and frankincense that drifted up from nearby bushes. Beneath the canopy of stars, the world seemed hushed, as though nature itself bowed in reverence to the holy journey unfolding upon its surface.

Mary's breath came softly, measured and even, though deep within her, a storm stirred. The child she carried was not merely any child, but the promised Messiah, the one long foretold by prophets whose scrolls had shaped generations with sacred words. The weight of this knowledge pressed gently upon her spirit even as the physical burden of travel pressed against her body. She knew that hardship lay ahead, but her heart was anchored by faith, and a quiet strength emanated from her that no mortal trial could quench.

Joseph, often vigilant, scanned the horizon for any sign of trouble. Not simply out of concern for safety, but because he too bore a great responsibility, not only to protect Mary but to safeguard the divine mystery entrusted to their care. His mind wrestled continually with the weight of this calling; a humble carpenter, yet chosen by the Most High to be the earthly guardian of the Savior. His footsteps were steady, deliberate, not hurried, for haste could raise dust and draw unwelcome eyes, yet not so slow as to delay the fulfillment of the Law, which demanded that every man return to his ancestral town to be registered.

As the night deepened, the chill intensified, creeping into bones and stiffening joints. Joseph produced a small bundle of dried figs and bread and carefully broke pieces to share. The simple repast was eaten in silence, the quiet communion speaking more than words ever could. The presence of hunger was a stark reminder of their mortal frailty, yet neither complaint nor despair found purchase in their hearts. Every hardship was but a step toward an unimaginable purpose, the dawn from which salvation itself would rise.

Faint sounds filtered through the stillness: distant bleating of sheep tended by a lone shepherd, the soft murmur of a far-off village preparing for the night. Occasionally, the faint jingle of harness bells from a passing caravan would remind them that life continued around them, ordinary and unremarked, even as their own journey bore eternal significance. The landscape bore the patina of time, ancient stones, weathered caves, olive trees gnarled with age, as if all creation had been waiting, watching for this moment.

Mary's hand rested lightly on her swollen belly, feeling the subtle movements of the child within; a delicate, secret rhythm that spoke of new life and divine promise. She whispered prayers under her breath, words of praise and supplication mingling with the cold night air. Though the road was long and the night bitter, an inner warmth glowed brightly, hope wrapped in flesh, a tangible shalom ready to enter the broken world.

The journey was not merely physical; it was a crossing between worlds, between the old covenant of law and sacrifice and the new covenant of grace and redemption. Every step echoed with the weight of sacred history and the dawn of a new salvation. Joseph's heart was a fortress of faith, his trust in God's word unshaken by the uncertainties and dangers that lay not far beyond the horizon. He drew strength also from Mary's serene courage, the calm in her face a balm against the hardships that would yet come.

As they neared Bethlehem, the twinkle of firelight from distant homes began to punctuate the darkness, warm beacons in the endless night. Yet, these same lights spoke also of no vacancies and crowded streets; the influx of others returning for registration pressed against familiar thresholds, turning once welcoming doors into barred gates. The thought of arrival brought a new kind of tension, yet Mary's soft sigh was not one of weariness but of acceptance; it was the final step of their pilgrimage, the moment foretold from the days of old.

The dusty road seemed to stretch endlessly, but then the silhouette of Bethlehem's stone walls emerged against the sky, a beloved town warmed by history, yet momentarily cold to the needs of strangers.

Joseph's voice broke the silence as he spoke quietly to Mary of the lineage of David, of the prophets who had spoken of this place as the birthplace of the Messianic King. The irony was not lost on either of them, the King of Kings would come forth not from palatial halls but from humble surroundings, a manger that smelled of hay and animal breath.

The air grew heavier with a mixture of exhaustion and imminence. Mary's hands trembled briefly, and Joseph instinctively steadied the donkey. The pulse of the child within was steady, a beating drum that echoed the heartbeat of humanity itself. The night's chill wrapped them in humble garments, but their spirits burned bright with an eternal flame, a light that shadows could not extinguish.

Finally, as the first faint blush of dawn crept along the eastern horizon, they reached the outskirts of Bethlehem. The sleepy town began to stir with laborers and merchants, but for Joseph and Mary, there was still no place to rest. The inns were full, filled with relatives and others who had come for the census. Yet in the midst of rejection and weariness, a simple stable was offered, its dusty warmth a humble cradle for the King. It was in that sacred, modest shelter that the journey would find its destination, and the promise written in prophecy would become flesh and dwell among men.

Thus, the journey to the manger was a tapestry woven from threads of hardship and hope, of earthly frailty and divine resolve. Mary and Joseph traversed not only the rough terrain of Judea but the profound intersection of heaven's will and human obedience. Their footsteps remain a testament to faith's quiet strength and the mystery of grace descending into the night, the silent night when Emmanuel came to dwell with us, the God who pierced the darkness with eternal light.

The Nativity Scene: Wonder in Humility

The night was silent, save for the faint rustling of straw and the quiet murmurs of a mother cradling her newborn child. In the humble stable in Bethlehem, the nativity scene unfolded, a tableau both simple and sublime, where heaven's whispered promises met the stark reality of earth's humility. Here, in this lowly place, amid the mingling scents of hay and animals, the world's Redeemer had come forth, wrapped in swaddling clothes and laid in a manger, an instrument once meant for feeding cattle, now transformed into an altar of divine mystery.

The soft glow of starlight filtered through the cracks in the stable's wooden beams, casting a gentle radiance that seemed to pulse with life. Each beam, knotted and worn, bore witness to countless seasons of rain and sunshine, but on this night, they bore witness to a greater marvel, the birth of Emmanuel, God with us. The light refracted upon the rough-hewn timbers, scattering into a thousand tiny points like a celestial crown encircling the sacred child.

The manger itself, a crude feeding trough fashioned from hardened wood, was covered with a bed of straw. The straw's roughness was softened by its golden hue and by the tender presence resting upon it. One could almost feel the faint creak of the brittle stalks, each one a whisper of the earth's bounty, now repurposed to support the infant King. The humble setting was a stark contrast to the reverent destiny unfolding within it. The foal's hay mingled with the delicate warmth radiating from the child, tying together the earthly and the divine in silent harmony.

Mary sat close by, the light of the small fire dancing across her face, highlighting the exhaustion mingled with awe in her eyes. Her hands, still marked by the toil of the journey from Nazareth, gently touched the baby's tiny fingers. It was a hand as small and fragile as a blossom, yet it held within it the power to redeem the world. Mary's heart was full, she was a woman who had been visited by angels, told of promises long foretold, now seeing them made flesh before her eyes. She whispered quiet praises, words that would have echoed softly if not for the stillness enveloping all.

Joseph, likewise weary, stood sentinel nearby, his figure cast in the shadows, humble and resolute. His role was that of protector, guardian of the divine child and his mother. Though questions may have lingered in his heart, in this moment, his focus was singular: the safety and well-being of this son, this hope born into their midst. The steady rise and fall of his breath kept time with the infant's soft coos and sighs, tying them together in a shared existence that was both earthly and eternal.

Beyond the immediate scene, angelic presences hovered, silent, unseen by many yet undeniably present. These beings, messengers of God's glory, lingered at the edges of the stable like shadows merging with the miraculous light. Their presence was profound and reverent; no trumpets blared, no grand fanfare disrupted the humble peace. Rather, they watched with an awe befitting the unfolding of the divine plan, their folded wings shimmering faintly in the star-strewn darkness.

The air was thick with a sense of wonder, an ineffable merging of heaven and earth, the infinite becoming enfleshed within a child who knew nothing of the power surrounding him. All creation seemed to hold its breath. The animals, accustomed to the everyday rhythms of the stable, huddled close to their newfound companion. The ox and the ass, emblematic and humble, shared the space without need for words, their warm breaths a steady reminder of life's persistence across all creatures.

This scene fulfills the ancient prophecies. Isaiah had foreseen a child born to us, a son given, whose name is Wonderful, Counselor, The Mighty God, The Everlasting Father, The Prince of Peace. Here and now, beneath a cool sky lit by the guiding star, the words of the prophets echo with fresh reality. The Messiah, the Anointed One, had come disguised in simplicity but crowned in significance.

Mary's thoughts wandered to the words she had kept in her heart, scriptures she had heard since youth, promises carried by her people for generations. She recalled the angel's greeting, "Hail, thou that art highly favored, the Lord is with thee." And now the Lord was indeed with them, not as thunder from heaven, but as a helpless babe, fragile and tiny, His divinity veiled in swaddling clothes. The paradox was staggering: the King of Kings lying in a manger, dependent on human care. Yet this humility was the very vehicle of salvation, the pathway through which grace would enter the world.

Joseph, though less given to words, felt the weight of responsibility tempered by quiet faith. He had obeyed the angel's visitation in dreams, had taken Mary as his wife despite perplexing circumstances. Now, as he looked upon the child, he saw a future wrought not only from earthly toil but from divine purpose. The child's eyes flickered open, reflecting the starlight like twin lamps of hope. Joseph was reminded of the psalmist's words: "Thou hast turned for me my mourning into dancing: thou hast put off my sackcloth, and girded me with gladness." Though the road ahead promised challenges, this night shone with an eternal gladness.

The glow from the fire was faint but persistent, its flames flickering against the faces gathered near. Mary brushed a stray lock from the child's forehead, the roughness of her palm juxtaposed with the silky softness of his hair. She felt the rise and fall of his breathing, a rhythm that echoed the life pulse of the entire cosmos. In the stillness of that night, time itself seemed suspended, the ordinary framed by the extraordinary.

Outside, the world was unaware, or rather unknowing. Only a few shepherds, tending flocks on the nearby hills, were about to be drawn into the narrative that would forever alter history. The heavens would soon ring with the angelic proclamation of peace and goodwill. But for now, the stable remained a sanctuary of quiet sanctity, a crucible where the greatest gift had been laid in the simplest terms.

The textures of this scene, the fragrant hay yielding softly beneath gentle hands, the warmth radiating from a mother's embrace, the aged wood absorbing the flickering light, come alive when read slowly, prayerfully. It is a holy intersection where the divine chooses frailty, glory cloaked in lowliness. This union of heaven and earth in the manger is the profound mystery of incarnation: that God condescends to our condition, entering our world not with pomp, but with humility.

Silent testimonies surround this moment. The stable's stones, cold and unyielding, cradle a warmth that can kindle the coldest heart. The stillness of the night, punctuated only by subtle murmurs and gentle sighs, is charged with expectancy, a latent power that will ripple through centuries. Every element, the rough straw, the tender touch, the shimmering starlight, acts as a witness to a love so great it stoops low to dwell among us.

The presence of the angels, though unseen by most, is felt in the sacred atmosphere. They hover like invisible guardians, their ethereal light mingling with the earthly glow, their silence proclaiming the profundity of the event. Their wings, magnificent yet folded, remind us that even heavenly beings stand in hushed reverence before the miracle unfolding below.

In this moment, obedience, faith, love, and hope are embodied in Mary and Joseph's watchful presence. They are the earthly vessels sustaining the divine life, participants in a story that will transcend time and touch every soul. Their expressions are etched with a combination of humility and awe, weariness and joy, acceptance and wonder.

As the child lies wrapped in swaddling clothes, the darkness outside contrasts sharply with the illumination within. The stars above, witnesses to the promise made long ago, sparkle with renewed brilliance. The world breathes anew, the light entering darkness and the darkness not comprehending it. Bethlehem, a city unassuming and small, becomes the birthplace of light eternal, where wonder is found not in grandeur but in humility.

This scene remains a timeless reminder that glory most often comes veiled in simplicity, that the heart of God beats strongest in the place of meekness. The manger, transformed from a simple feeding place into a sanctuary of salvation, echoes through every generation. Here, in this holy place, the divine and human embrace, and through that embrace, hope is born.

Shepherds and the Angelic Chorus

The quiet hills surrounding Bethlehem held a profound stillness as night descended, punctuated only by the occasional crackling of the shepherds' fires. These were men accustomed to solitude, their lives intimately intertwined with the rugged landscape, guiding their flocks beneath the vast expanse of the starlit sky. The low murmurs of woolly sheep, the rustling of dry grass, and the occasional bleating echoed amidst the peaceful darkness. Yet, on this night, the ordinary was about to be shattered by an extraordinary revelation that would illuminate the hearts of simple men and echo through eternity.

The air was cold and crisp, a gentle chill that brushed against the skin and made the breath curl into small clouds. Every sound seemed sharper in the coolness, the crack of a twig underfoot, the rustle of a bird startled into flight, the distant murmur of the village lights nestled below. The quiet majesty of the night held an expectant quality, almost as if creation itself paused in anticipation. The shepherds sat around their modest fires, faces half-shrouded in shadow, eyes lifted to the tapestry of twinkling stars above. Their work, tedious and steady, awaited no herald; yet fate had decreed that these humble watchers would be the first to witness the dawn of a new covenant.

Suddenly, the darkness was pierced by an explosion of light. A radiant figure, a messenger of God, appeared in the shepherds' midst like the sun breaking through storm clouds. The flame of their fires seemed to pale in comparison as the angelic countenance shone with an unearthly brilliance, radiating peace yet commanding reverence. The shepherds were seized by a tremor of awe and fear so profound that their bodies stiffened, breath caught in their throats as the glow washed over them like a rushing tide. It was as though the very atmosphere vibrated with a sacred energy, an invisible power that spoke directly to the soul.

The angel's voice broke the silence, a sound both thunderous and gentle, woven with the sweetness of a lullaby and the authority of divine decree. "Fear not," he proclaimed, a phrase that carried the weight of reassurance and hope, dispelling the shadows of dread that threatened to overwhelm those gathered. "For behold, I bring you good tidings of great joy, which shall be to all people. For unto you is born this day in the city of David a Savior, who is Christ the Lord." The words hung in the night air, shimmering like stars born anew, each syllable a beacon of light that illuminated the shepherds' hearts from within.

Then, as if summoned by the angel's declaration, the heavens themselves seemed to open, and a multitude of the heavenly host appeared, filling the night sky with radiant brilliance. The angelic chorus burst forth in glorious harmony, their voices weaving a tapestry of sound and light that transcended human understanding. The music was neither merely heard nor seen but experienced in a fusion of senses, a symphony that blended the radiance of dawn with the purest tones of celestial song. It was as if the very essence of joy took form and danced across the firmament, touching all who bore witness with an ineffable peace.

The melody soared and sank, a luminous wave that broke against the shepherds' souls, filling their hearts with a swelling tide of awe and wonder. The brightness of the angels' presence painted the night with hues untold, colors that no earthly eye could discern but that shimmered vividly in the spiritual vision granted to these humble men. Each note carried an ethereal glow, a resonance that lingered long after the last refrain faded into the silence of the sleeping fields. "Glory to God in the highest," they sang, their voices radiant beams that pierced the firmament, "and on earth peace, goodwill toward men."

In the midst of this divine spectacle, the shepherds' terror gradually gave way to reverent comprehension. Their initial trembling, born of the sanctity of the encounter, softened into a profound joy that radiated through their beings. The harsh contours of their arduous lives faded, replaced by the warm light of hope and faith. The angelic annunciation was not merely a message but a transformative touch; it rewrote the narrative of their existence, elevating their simple, rugged hearts to holders of sacred trust.

With the angelic host vanished as suddenly as they had come, the night returned to its serene silence, but the fire in the shepherds' souls blazed brighter than any earthly flame. They exchanged glances, their eyes shining with a newfound conviction, voices trembling as they spoke of what they had witnessed. The journey from fear to faith was marked not solely by intellectual assent but by a palpable shift in their spirits, where doubt once resided now blossomed a luminous certainty.

Rising from the hay and dirt beneath them, the shepherds moved with a sense of urgency and reverence, leaving behind their fires to traverse the cool wilderness toward Bethlehem. The rough terrain that had been the backdrop of their daily toil now became a path of pilgrimage, each step echoing the heartbeat of a world on the cusp of redemption. The night air, once filled with uncertainty, now carried the notes of anticipation, as if all nature itself conspired to guide them toward the miraculous.

Their shadows stretched long beneath the silver moon, fleeting echoes of their humble faith made manifest. The shepherds pressed onward, hearts ablaze with the good news that had been entrusted into their hands. As they drew closer to the manger where the infant King lay wrapped in swaddling clothes, the words of the angel reverberated within them, transforming their fear into worship, their doubt into unshakable devotion.

Through this tender encounter, the divine had chosen the lowly and the meek to receive the glad tidings. The shepherds, custodians of the night, became heralds of the dawn, bearers of a story that would transcend generations. Their testimony, born from a night of radiant angels and trembling awe, would spread the light of hope across the world, a beacon for all who sought salvation in the Christ child.

In the quiet aftermath, as the fires dwindled to embers and the first pale blush of dawn crept across the hills, the shepherds returned not as mere men but as witnesses to eternity. Their souls, forever touched by the angelic chorus, bore the mark of divine revelation. Through the sensory tapestry of light, sound, and the sacred encounters beneath the Bethlehem sky, the shepherds' journey from fear to faith stands as a testament to the transformative power of God's Word made flesh, a story whispered in the silence, sung by angels, and embraced by humble hearts across the ages.

The Baptism and the Holy Dove

John the Baptist: The Voice Crying in the Wilderness

In the vast expanse of Judea's wilderness, where rocky cliffs meet barren sands and the breath of the desert winds whispers through olive groves, a solitary figure stands out against the rugged landscape. Clad in clothing of camel's hair and a leather girdle, John the Baptist prowls the wilderness valleys with a voice that cuts through the stillness like a trumpet call. The wilderness, inhospitable and raw, is both stage and symbol for a ministry that resounds with urgency and divine mandate, a clarion call for repentance and renewal.

John's ministry emerges like a living flame amid the desolation, a vivid contrast between the stark wilderness and the vibrant urgency of his message. The desert, with its barrenness and solitude, reflects the spiritual wasteland that John proclaims must be cleansed. There is no gentle whisper but a voice crying out in the wilderness, calling the people of Israel to prepare the way of the Lord, to make straight His paths. In this solitude of rocky crags and dry riverbeds, the echo of prophetic necessity rings out, the time is near for redemption; the Kingdom of God is at hand.

From the earliest dawn, the wilderness becomes a gathering place where multitudes flock, drawn by the magnetic power of John's preaching. From villages and towns, from cities swarming with cynicism, people come, tax collectors, soldiers, Pharisees, Sadducees, peasants, and priests alike. Each soul comes burdened by the weight of sin and the longing for purification. They come to hear the voice that rends the silence, to be touched by the waters that cleanse, washing away the filth of transgression and igniting a spark of new life.

John's message is uncompromising. With prophetic zeal, he denounces the hardness of heart, the complacency with evil, and the hypocrisy lurking within the religious elite. "O generation of vipers," he declares, "who hath warned you to flee from the wrath to come?" His words fall like stones upon hardened ground, yet in their piercing force, there lies mercy and hope. Repent ye: for the kingdom of heaven is at hand. The wilderness is transformed into a courtroom where harsh condemnation and boundless grace collide.

At the heart of John's ministry is the ritual of baptism, a sacred, symbolic act of purification and renewal. The flowing waters of the Jordan River become a visible sign of inward repentance, a washing away of sin, a preparation for the coming Christ. The image of water flowing, cleansing, and restoring courses through the narrative of John's mission, embodying the spiritual transformation he proclaims. The Jordan's waters not only cleanse the outward man but signify a rebirth unto righteousness and faith.

John himself stands as the ultimate forerunner, bridging the chasm between the old covenant and the dawning new age. He is the Elijah who was promised to come before the great and dreadful day of the Lord. His role is essential, preparing the spiritual soil for the coming Messiah by turning hearts from sin to holiness. John's wilderness ministry is both a fulfillment of ancient prophecy and the ignition of a new divine purpose.

The landscape of John's world is harsh yet fertile in meaning. Hills and valleys echo the ups and downs of the human soul. The wilderness, once a place of exile and desolation for the children of Israel, becomes the hallowed ground for repentance and renewal. The starkness of the environment mirrors the stripping away of worldly attachments and the embracing of divine truth. Each cry of John is a summons to desert the false comforts of sin and enter into the refreshing, though sometimes challenging, depths of repentance.

Crowds gather by the banks of the Jordan, their garments soaking, their souls searching. The muffled sounds of feet shuffling through sand and stone mingle with the murmurs of expectation. There is an electric tension as sinners bow their heads beneath the flowing water, confessing guilt, embracing humility, and emerging cleansed. The water that envelops them symbolizes both judgment and mercy, death to sin and life to righteousness.

John's physical appearance, wild hair, rugged garment, diet of locusts and wild honey, reflects a life entirely committed to the prophetic. He is a living prophecy, a man set apart from the comforts and distractions of civilization, wholly devoted to the singular task of heralding the Christ. His ascetic lifestyle underscores the urgency and seriousness of his message, calling others to similarly forsake sin and worldly indulgence in favor of renewal.

The cries that issue from the wilderness are more than mere words; they are a summons echoing through time, calling every generation to confront sin and to prepare a way for the Lord's coming. John's voice, strong and unwavering, slices through spiritual complacency. He demands fruit worthy of repentance; mere lip service will not suffice. The axe is already laid at the root of the trees, he warns. The coming fire will purge what is unworthy, and only that which is true and pure will endure.

John's proclamation is not just a call to individual repentance but a summons to collective transformation. He addresses social structures, challenging tax collectors to exact no more than that which is appointed and soldiers to live with honesty and integrity without extortion or false accusation. His message travels beyond personal sin to the very fabric of societal repentance and holiness.

This wilderness prophet's words resonate deeply because they connect the present moment with ancient promises. Isaiah's prophecy is fulfilled: "The voice of one crying in the wilderness, Prepare ye the way of the Lord, make his paths straight." John's ministry is the tangible, living fulfillment of this promise. It anchors the people in hope, a hope grounded not in political revolution but in the approaching reign of God.

In the midst of this wilderness setting, where life and death, judgment and mercy, desolation and hope intertwine, John the Baptist crafts a ministry that is as raw and real as the land he inhabits. His voice is a lifeline for the weary and lost, signaling the beginning of a new covenant of grace. The wilderness, once a place of exile, now rings with words of promise. The baptizer's call is loud and clear: prepare ye the way of the Lord.

As the crowds gather and John immerses repentant souls into the cleansing waters, the anticipation grows for the one who is coming after him, one mightier, whose shoes he is unworthy to bear. John's ministry fades into the background, yet it remains foundational, the necessary precursor to the great work that Jesus Christ will accomplish. Without John's voice crying in the wilderness, the transformative power of the baptism of Jesus would lose its profound context.

Thus, John the Baptist stands as a pivotal figure in the divine narrative, a prophetic bridge connecting law and grace, judgment and mercy. His wilderness ministry is a beacon that lights the darkened path of humanity, urging all to turn from sin, embrace repentance, and prepare their hearts for the Lord's advent. In his voice, in his garments, in the baptismal waters, the continuity of divine purpose flows uninterrupted, forging the way for salvation to come.

The voice crying in the wilderness still echoes each time baptismal waters touch a repentant soul, each time someone yields to the call for transformation. John's legacy is not only historical but eternal, for he embodies the persistent call from God that repentance is the path to life, and that preparation of the heart is necessary to receive the King who comes to save. In the wilderness, amid the rocks and sands, amidst the clamoring crowds seeking redemption, John's ministry stands immortal, a beacon and a bridge to the wondrous work of Christ's baptism and the descent of the Holy Dove.

Jesus Steps Into the Waters

The day was marked by a tranquil stillness, as if all of creation held its breath in anticipation. Along the banks of the Jordan River, the air shimmered with the veiled promise of something profound unfolding. The gentle daylight filtered through a canopy of leaves, dappling the soft earth beneath, mingling with the ever-present mist rising from the river's surface. This mist, ethereal and fleeting, swirled in delicate eddies above the water, where the current moved steadily, the clear river flowing with a quiet dignity, as if it too was a participant in the sacred moment that was about to transpire.

Jesus approached the water's edge with humble resolve, His feet sinking softly into the cool, damp sand and pebbles. The sensation of the earth beneath Him was grounding, a quiet reminder of the humanity He embraced, even as divinity shone from His countenance. His simple garment, untouched by the cares of the world, hung lightly, swaying gently with every motion. The atmosphere thickened with an invisible weight, a sacred hush that stilled voices and silenced thoughts. Those who watched felt the pall of serene expectation drape over the gathering, as if time itself slowed to witness the confluence of heaven and earth.

The water beckoned, a living symbol of purity, renewal, and the ancient rites of cleansing. It glided over stones and ripples, smooth as silk, carrying reflections of sky and trembling leaves upon its surface. To step into it was to enter a realm where the physical and the spiritual converged, where the ordinary was transformed through an act of profound submission and trust. Jesus, fully aware of the magnitude of this moment, prepared to immerse Himself in the waters that had long symbolized repentance and new beginnings for the people who frequented these banks.

As He stepped forward, the coolness of the river greeted Him, a crisp sensation that lapped gently against His skin, a refreshment that belied the weight of the worldly burdens He bore silently. The feeling was at once renewing and grounding. Water, ever mutable and persistent, wrapped around Him like a silken embrace, flowing over hair and forehead, cascading down His form, washing away not in judgment but in the grace of an unspoken covenant between the Creator and His creation.

The immersion itself was a sacred rite, rich with layered meaning. This was not a mere act of physical cleansing, but a profound symbol of identification and mission. By submitting to the waters, Jesus aligned Himself with the very people He came to serve. Though without sin, He chose the path of humility, descending into the waters that had for ages borne the stains of human imperfection, that had welcomed penitent souls seeking renewal. His baptism would serve as the threshold into His ministry, a visible declaration of the divine purpose that would soon unfold.

Around the riverbank, the murmurs of the crowd fell silent as eyes fixed upon this singular moment. The rustle of leaves and the soft rush of the Jordan were joined now by a collective stillness that seemed to cradle the scene itself. Every detail, the measured swirl of water, the steady breath of the One in the river, the vapor rising like a veil between earth and sky, woven together in timeless harmony. It was as if the heavens had opened in quiet witness, the very air imbued with expectation, sanctified by the presence of the One who was both man and God.

In this immersion, the narrative of Jesus's life crystallized. It was a baptism not only of water but of identity; not only a cleansing but a consecration. The silence spoke volumes, the loudest declaration that words alone could never capture. Here, the God-man embraced the fullness of His humanity, submitting to the humble rite of baptism that confessed the frailty and brokenness of human existence. Yet, in so doing, He simultaneously embraced the divine mission of salvation, reconciliation, and restoration.

The Kingdom of Heaven, though invisible in this mist-wreathed moment, was made manifest in the very act of stepping into the waters. Scriptural echoes resonated through the air, as if the words of the prophets and the rhythm of the sacred texts themselves were etched into the flowing river, calling to those who would listen with the heart. Isaiah's voice, foretelling the Servant who would bear the sins of many; the psalms that sang of God's steadfast love that renews the soul; the ancient promises of the Messiah who would bring justice and peace, all found their living fulfillment in this gentle, holy drowning and rising.

To the beholder, it was a visual and spiritual symphony. The water, clear and cleansing; the sky, unraveling light through vapor; the expectancy that held the breaths of witnesses, all combined to invite reflection upon the solemn beauty of divine acceptance. In this baptism, human humility met divine affirmation. To deny the self and submit to the waters was to open the soul to the currents of grace that would carry Jesus forward upon His path. The sacred dove, often unseen but always near, hovered silently in the ambiance, an unseen seal upon this sacred act.

For Jesus, this was both an ending and a beginning. It was the end of hidden preparation and the beginning of open proclamation. His first step into the water was a step onto the public stage of ministry, a real act of obedience that heralded the coming kingdom. Every droplet that shimmered and trickled from His form bore testimony of surrender and purpose. Each ripple cast upon the river spoke silently of the waves of transformation He would bring upon the world.

The immersion, rendered in rich sensory detail, invites us to contemplate not only the external elements but the internal drama. To feel the cool water sliding over skin, to see the mist swirl and curl above the river, to hear the near silence punctuated by the gentle rush of currents, is to participate in the moment. It is to draw near and glimpse the profound mystery where God's chosen One steps fully into His vocation and identity. It is a baptism not only of Jesus but, metaphorically, for all who seek to know the weight and wonder of surrendering to divine will.

The sacred currents carried Him, the living water that both symbolized and enacted the spiritual cleansing necessary for all who would enter into a renewed covenant with God. Yet in Jesus's case, the baptism took on a singular meaning: He stood not only as the Sinless Lamb but as the one who would soon bear in Himself the sins of the world. His immersion was the threshold at which the invisible plan of salvation was made visible, a plan that began with obedience and humility and would culminate in ultimate sacrifice and triumphant resurrection.

As He rose from the waters, droplets glittered like jewels in the sunlight, a radiant fringe signifying new birth and divine approval. The river seemed to hold its breath briefly, then gently resumed its ancient song. The crowd, stirred from silence, felt the tremor of something momentous. The heavens themselves, as recorded in the accounts, opened, and a voice spoke, a voice that declared the identity and mission of this Man who had just emerged from the waters.

The gravity of this inauguration remains timeless. In the gentle flow of the Jordan, where the water glides like silk and the mist rises in a veil of mystery, readers encounter the spiritual awakening that baptized Jesus into His earthly mission. The moment remains a foundational chapter in the story of redemption, a holy crossing where heaven and earth touch, where God's voice rings out to confirm God's Son, and where human humility is embraced and transformed by divine acceptance.

Here lies the invitation not only to witness history but to enter into the heart of faith itself. When Jesus steps into the waters, He steps into a new reality, one where His divinity is affirmed, His mission is embraced, and the path to salvation is inaugurated. This image, vivid and compelling, calls forth from the reader a participation in the sacred narrative, to perceive and honor the gravity and grace of the baptism, an initiation not only of a man but of the Redemption itself.

In this sanctified immersion, the interplay of natural elements and divine presence invites us to linger in the moment, to taste the coolness of the holy water, to breathe in the mist, and to sense the stillness of expectation. It beckons us to remember that every act of obedience, every surrender to grace, carries within it the power to transform and renew. Just as the water once flowed over Jesus, washing and anointing, so too can it flow over us, the waters of baptism, faith, and spiritual awakening, inviting us into the same mystery of acceptance, mission, and new life.

Thus, the story of Jesus stepping into the waters is not merely an event frozen in time but a living truth stretched across the centuries. It is a call to humility and purpose, a symbol of the divine embrace that covers even the humblest soul. It is the sacred moment when the Son of God condescended to walk the path of sinners, receiving the baptism of repentance not for Himself but for the sake of all mankind. This passage into the waters sets the stage for the unfolding drama of redemption, where grace flows deeper than the Jordan and mercy reaches to the farthest horizons of the human heart.

The reader, immersed in the sensory richness and spiritual depth of this moment, is thus invited to step forward in faith, into a river of encounter where the eternal meets the temporal, the divine touches the human, and the grace of God cascades like living water over every life ready to be renewed.

The Spirit Descends: The Dove's Silent Song

Amidst the river's gentle flow and the solemn tranquility of the moment, the scene unfolds with a profound and radiant simplicity, an image that will resonate through the ages, whispered in the hearts of believers and etched into the tapestry of sacred history. It is here, at the very commencement of Jesus's public ministry, that heaven's interaction with earth is made manifest in a singular and breathtaking event: the descent of the Holy Spirit, taking the form of a dove.

The air hangs heavy with expectation as John the Baptist, steadfast in his prophetic mission, prepares to baptize the One from Nazareth. The waters of the Jordan ripple quietly beneath the overcast sky, a mirror reflecting both the solemnity and the significance of what is to come. In the midst of this sacred act, a luminous image emerges, a dove, as if carved from pure light and gentleness, descending slowly from the heavens.

This gentle bird, the holy dove, carries with it a profound symbolism that transcends its earthly simplicity. The Spirit's descent is no mere happenstance; it is a divine emissary crossing the veil between the celestial and the terrestrial. The dove's silent song, an eternal hymn of peace and purity, echoes softly in the spiritual senses rather than in the audible world. Its wings, outstretched and embracing, symbolize an encompassing grace that protects and nurtures the One who stands in the water, anointed at last for His holy mission.

The image of the dove is laden with meaning, thrumming with the depths of spiritual truth. In biblical tradition, the dove is a symbol of peace, an emblem of purity unspoiled by the corruption of the world. It recalls the ancient story of Noah, when the dove returns with the olive leaf, signaling the renewal of the earth and the promise of restoration. Here, at the baptism of Jesus, the dove brings a similar message: a sign that the age of reconciliation between God and man is dawning, a promise that salvation will flow as surely as the river's currents.

The dove is also an unmistakable symbol of the Holy Spirit, the divine presence and power that moves invisibly yet irresistibly through all creation. Its descent carries the weight of divine endorsement, a heavenly affirmation of Jesus's identity and mission. The Holy Spirit, in descending like a dove, reveals the intimate communion of the Trinity: the Father, speaking from heaven; the Son, standing in the water; and the Spirit, alighting gently upon Him. Each Person of the Godhead is present, united in the moment, marking the inauguration of the Messiah's public work.

As the dove descends, the atmosphere is suffused with sacred presence, an ineffable holy stillness that envelops the riverbank. The world seems to hold its breath; time itself appears to pause. Light and silence intermingle; a divine symphony plays not upon earthly instruments, but in the spiritual realms where sound, light, and quietude blend seamlessly. The brightness of the Spirit's descent fills the air with a celestial radiance, illuminating the countenance of Jesus in a way that words can barely convey. It is a revelation not just of identity, but of divine purpose, a beacon set ablaze in human history, calling all who hear to a deeper faith.

Suddenly, amidst this divine quietude, a voice, pure and penetrating as the morning sun, pierces the heavens and earth alike. This voice, the voice of the Almighty, proclaims in unmistakable clarity: "This is my beloved Son, in whom I am well pleased." It is a voice that baptizes not in water, but in authority; it seals the moment with a sacred decree. Each word echoes as both confirmation and invitation. Jesus is the Son set apart, the chosen bearer of God's redemptive plan, the One who will fulfill all that has been promised.

The pronouncement carries with it immeasurable weight. It is a divine benediction that brings everything into focus and infuses the scene with renewed meaning. For those present, it fills hearts with awe; for generations yet unborn, it becomes a cornerstone of faith. It is as though heaven's very voice has stooped to affirm the earthly Messiah, testifying to the fulfillment of prophecy and the dawn of a new covenant.

This sublime moment marks more than a ceremonial rite; it symbolizes the consecration of Jesus for the work that lies ahead. It is here that the Son of God, fully human and fully divine, receives the Holy Spirit as His power, the Spirit that will guide, strengthen, and uphold Him throughout His ministry. It is the anointing that initiates His journey of teaching, healing, and ultimately, sacrifice.

As this scene lingers in the soul's eye, the harmony of elements, the delicate flapping of wings, the hushed breath of the wind, the piercing clarity of the Father's voice, and the rippling embrace of the water create a spiritual fabric that wraps around the moment, sealing it in eternity. It is a symphony without sound, a painting without pigment, yet in its silent eloquence, it speaks louder than any earthly spectacle.

Through this divine encounter, the world is forever changed. The Spirit's descent is not merely a confirmation but a promise: that through Jesus, the peace and purity represented by the dove will come to dwell among men. The heavens declare their approval, inspiring awe, awakening hope, and kindling a renewal of faith that will ripple through centuries.

In this silent, radiant moment, the Spirit's song, the dove's silent song, beckons all who listen to step into the light of new understanding and grace. It calls forth a response of worship and wonder, inviting us to walk alongside the Son of God as He sets forth on the path appointed for Him from before the foundation of the world.

Thus, the Spirit descends, not as a mere symbol to be admired at a distance, but as an active presence, living, breathing, and forever interwoven with the ministry of Jesus. The dove's silent song resounds still, echoing through the corridors of history, speaking peace into restless souls, and carrying the hope of divine fellowship to all who dare to believe.

Teaching on the Mount

The Gathering of the Multitudes

The morning dawned gently over the hills of Galilee, casting a soft, golden light that filtered through the leaves of ancient olive trees. The air was sweetened by the wildflowers blooming in the cracks of sun-warmed stone, and the earth beneath carried the simple scent of dust and fresh grass, still moist with last night's dew. This hillside, rising modestly but with a gracious sweep toward the east, was alive with movement, for multitudes were gathering, drawn as much by curiosity as by hope, to hear the man known as Jesus of Nazareth.

From the valley below and distant paths winding through olive groves and fig orchards, men, women, and children ascended the gentle slope. Some came hastening, eager for a word of hope or healing; others walked slowly, their pace measured by age or thought. The mix was diverse, a mosaic of humanity, each person carrying the weight of their own lives and longing, their faces etched with stories both spoken and silent.

Among the crowds were fishermen, their hands rough from nets and oars, eyes bright with expectant wonder. They came from the nearby Sea of Galilee, where the morning mist still hovered. There were also the scribes and Pharisees of the towns, clad in their distinctive robes, curious yet cautious, their gazes sharp as the folds of their garments. Women traveled in small groups, their attentive eyes shielding children or gently clasping hands, hoping to catch a glimpse of the Teacher whose words were said to heal the sick and calm the storm. The elderly shuffled forward, leaning upon staffs weathered by years, their faces lined with the wisdom and weariness of a lifetime spent in service to God and family.

At the front of the ascending hill, a simple place had been chosen. A large rock jutted from the earth, flat-topped and inviting, like a natural pulpit. Its surface caught the morning light, glowing softly, as if anointed for holy purpose. Nearby, a scattering of wild thyme and rosemary grew, filling the air with a pungent fragrance that mingled strangely with the fresher scents of the earth and olive leaves. This unadorned spot was now the gathering place for heaven and earth to meet, where spiritual truths would descend like dew to thirsty souls.

The crowd thickened as the sun rose higher. Children, fidgeting and shifting restlessly, squinted toward the rock, while mothers comforted them with soft murmurs. Young men, their tunics dusty from travel, leaned against olive trunks or perched on sun-warmed stones, their expressions a mixture of skepticism and yearning. Older women whispered to one another, their voices low but urgent, eager to know if this new Teacher might indeed fulfill the ancient promises to Israel.

The scene was alive with anticipation. The rustle of garments blended with the soft murmur of voices, creating a gentle hum over the hillside. Occasional birdcalls punctuated the stillness, a lark soaring above, a dove cooing from a distant tree. The atmosphere was charged, not with loud proclamations or fanfare, but with something far deeper: a collective breath held in longing.

Among the crowd, some sat quietly, their faces folded in prayer or thought, while others exchanged hopeful glances, as if sharing an unspoken question: Could this be the day when burdens would be lifted, when words spoken would scatter fear and doubt like chaff before the wind? The air was thick with spiritual expectancy, the kind that fills hearts on the brink of awakening.

Jesus stood upon the rock, his frame simple and unassuming, yet commanding a presence rooted not in power but in profound authority. His eyes swept over the assembly with tenderness and understanding, recognizing each face as unique, each soul as precious. He knew the trials behind their steps, the sickness, the grief, the poverty, the unmet yearning for peace. And he came not to condemn, but to call forth the heart of a new kingdom, where love would reign and the inward life be transformed.

In that moment, as the light caught his countenance and the olive branches swayed in a gentle breeze, the hillside seemed to hold its breath. This was not merely a gathering of people; it was a sacred assembly, a community formed by a shared hunger for truth and grace. Here, beneath the vast expanse of sky, heaven's wisdom was poised to descend, touching earth not with thunder but with gentle invitation.

The varying emotions among the listeners were as palpable as the warm sunlight. There was the woman who had endured many miscarriages, her heart heavy with silent sorrow, hoping for a blessing that seemed all but lost. Nearby, a young man wrestled with doubt, his mind torn between tradition and the stirring new ideas he had heard whispered in the marketplace. The elderly scribe, schooled in the letter of the law, watched carefully, his hands folded yet his posture tense, uncertain whether this man was friend or heretic. A mother cradled a child with a fevered brow, her prayer mixed with tears slipping silently down her cheeks.

Yet amid these varied hopes and doubts, a common thread bound them, their desire to hear the words of this Teacher whose reputation had spread like wildfire: words not of condemnation but of mercy, not of harsh judgment but of radical love. The people sensed that this was no ordinary gathering; something deeper stirred in the spirit of the crowd, a subtle stirring that awakened old longings for righteousness and peace.

As Jesus prepared to speak, no grand proclamation announced the moment. There were no trumpets, no heralds, only the natural chorus of the hillside and the expectant hush of many souls. It was as if the heavens and the earth conspired in a silent symphony to make this hour sacred.

Then, with a voice calm yet compelling, Jesus began. His words reached not only the ears but the hearts of the listeners. They were words of blessing, pronouncements on those often overlooked or cast aside. "Blessed are the poor in spirit: for theirs is the kingdom of heaven." The opening beatitude fell like gentle rain, moistening the dry soil of many hearts.

In these simple yet profound statements, the assembly felt the presence of a new covenant, an invitation into a kingdom where the last would be first, the meek would inherit the earth, and those who mourn would find comfort. The gathering, diverse in background and burden, was unified in this moment of revelation, their various hopes and doubts giving way to a shared glimpse of divine truth.

The morning sun climbed higher, yet the crowd remained fixed on the Teacher's every word. The hillside became a place where voices of heaven whispered to those of the dust, where ancient promises echoed afresh through timeless wisdom. The scents, the sounds, the gentle warmth, all became woven into the fabric of a sacred memory, a moment when heaven touched earth and opened wide a door to life everlasting.

Thus, the gathering of multitudes on that Galilean hillside was more than a mere assembly; it was a sacred convergence. Men and women from differing walks of life were drawn together not by force but by a longing stoked within their spirits. They came hungry, not merely for bread but for righteousness, not simply for healing but for hope, not only for instruction but for transformation. In the shadow of olive trees and beneath the eternal sky, they awaited the unfolding of the Sermon on the Mount, the teaching that would illuminate paths, bind wounds, and offer a new vision of God's kingdom come near.

Through the mingling of earth's rustic scents and the fresh dawn light, through the varied faces reflecting faith and frailty alike, the stage was set. The Teacher was ready to speak, his words to ripple through generations, calling all into a life marked by mercy, purity of heart, and peace. The gathering of the multitudes had become a holy assembly, a moment when heaven's wisdom graced the earth with gentle power, transforming the ordinary hillside into a hallowed ground of divine encounter.

The Beatitudes: Windows into Heaven

In the gentle rise of the hill, where the murmuring crowd gathered with eager anticipation, Jesus lifted His eyes toward heaven and began to speak words that would echo through the corridors of eternity. The Beatitudes, eight declarations of blessing, flowed from His lips like a clear and sparkling stream, each one a radiant lantern shedding light upon the weary and the hopeful alike. These sayings, simple yet profound, unfold like windows into heaven, inviting all who hear to glimpse the nature of God's kingdom and the character of those who belong to it.

"Blessed are the poor in spirit: for theirs is the kingdom of heaven." With this opening pronouncement, the heart of the message is tenderly revealed. The "poor in spirit" are not merely those who lack material wealth, but those who come to God in humility, recognizing their spiritual need and utter dependency upon Him. It is a beautiful paradox that poverty in spirit is the key to possessing the kingdom of heaven. The phrase beckons us to lay down pride and self-sufficiency, to embrace a posture of vulnerability before God. This blessing is an open invitation to the broken, the contrite, and the humble to take their rightful place in God's family.

To stand poor in spirit is to acknowledge that we have no claim to righteousness of our own, that every good thing is a gift from the hand of the Father. It is the gentle opening of a soul, like a flower unfolding its petals to the sun, ready to receive nourishment and life. The kingdom of heaven is promised to them, not as a distant dream, but as a present reality, a divine inheritance available now and forevermore.

"Blessed are they that mourn: for they shall be comforted." Here, mourning widens beyond sorrow for personal loss to encompass lament over sin, injustice, and the brokenness of a suffering world. It is the mourning born of a heart grieved by the weight of evil both in others and within ourselves. Yet, in this sadness, there is a tender hope: comfort. The promise of divine consolation is certain and compelling. The mourning soul is not abandoned to despair; instead, it finds refuge in the loving embrace of God, who tenderly heals and restores.

The spiritual significance of mourning lies in the transformation it triggers. When we mourn over sin, we are driven to repentance; when we lament the pain in the world, we are compelled toward compassion and action. The comfort that Jesus promises is not mere alleviation of pain but the profound peace that surpasses understanding, the balm that only God Himself can provide. As God's children, those who mourn do so not in isolation or without purpose but in the hope of renovation, their tears watering the soil in which joy and righteousness will grow.

"Blessed are the meek: for they shall inherit the earth." Meekness, often mistaken for weakness, is in truth a strength clothed in gentleness and self-control. The meek are those who refrain from asserting their own power arrogantly; they trust God's timing and sovereignty rather than their own force. This blessed state calls to mind the image of a lamb, quiet yet resolute, whose power lies in a humble spirit attuned to God's will.

In inheriting the earth, the meek receive not just physical territory but the fullness of God's provision and peace. The earth, marred by strife and greed, will one day be restored to those whose hearts are steady and pure. The meek do not seize their inheritance through conquest; rather, they claim it by faithful endurance and divine promise. Their reward is both immediate and eternal, as they live in harmony with creation and under the rule of the Prince of Peace.

"Blessed are they who hunger and thirst after righteousness, for they shall be filled." Hunger and thirst are primal needs, driving us toward sustenance with irresistible force. To hunger and thirst after righteousness is to possess an intense desire for justice, holiness, and right standing with God. This is not a casual yearning but a consuming appetite for what is good, true, and pleasing in the sight of the Almighty.

The promise that such longing will be satisfied is both comforting and assuring. Those who devote themselves to pursuing righteousness do so knowing that their efforts will not be in vain. God Himself will fill this deep craving with His presence and favor. The metaphor urges the reader to taste the sweetness of God's justice, to be refreshed not merely in body but at the deepest level of soul. There is a participatory aspect here, like drinking cool water on a parched day, the blessed find their souls restored and renewed in the pursuit of what God desires.

"Blessed are the merciful: for they shall obtain mercy." Mercy flows from the heart of God, who spared His people and reached out to the lost. To be merciful is to reflect this divine compassion to others through forgiveness, kindness, and practical aid. The merciful are those who soften hardness with grace, who bridge divides with empathy, and who reach out generously even when it costs them.

In obtaining mercy, the merciful experience the reciprocal nature of God's kingdom. The mercy they extend becomes the mercy they receive, a beautiful cycle of grace that sustains relationships and restores brokenness. This beatitude teaches that the attitude of the heart toward others colors the blessings that will be received from God. It calls for active love, a kindness that moves beyond sentiment to tangible acts of care. The merciful live in a community shaped by compassion, reflecting the heart of Christ Himself.

"Blessed are the pure in heart: for they shall see God." Purity of heart speaks to singular intention, clarity of motive, and the absence of deceit or corruption within one's inner life. The pure in heart are those whose affections and desires are directed solely toward God, whose gaze remains undivided even in a world filled with distraction and temptation.

The promise to see God is perhaps the most profound of all, for it speaks to intimate communion and the ultimate hope of believers. To see God is to enter into fuller revelation and understanding, to be drawn into the light of divine presence without obstruction. The metaphor of sight here is powerful: it implies clarity, truth, and the unveiling of what is hidden. Those with pure hearts will experience the reality of God's presence both now and in the age to come, their vision no longer clouded by sin or pretense but sharpened by love and holiness.

"Blessed are the peacemakers: for they shall be called the children of God." Peace is a treasure long sought by humanity, yet so often elusive. The peacemakers are those who actively pursue reconciliation and harmony, seeking not merely to avoid conflict but to establish justice, understanding, and unity. They bear the special identity of being called children of God, for in their work, they reflect the nature of the Father, who Himself is the God of peace.

To be a peacemaker is to participate in God's mission of restoration, to reach across barriers of hostility and division, bearing the imprint of divine love. This beatitude challenges the believer to step beyond passivity and to become agents of healing in a fractured world. Their reward is recognition as members of God's family, a familial title that confers dignity and responsibility.

"Blessed are they which are persecuted for righteousness' sake: for theirs is the kingdom of heaven." Persecution has been a constant companion of the faithful throughout history, and Jesus promises that those who suffer for justice and godliness are especially blessed. The kingdom of heaven belongs to them, affirming that their sacrifice and steadfastness are not overlooked.

This promise sustains believers in times of trial, reminding them that suffering has a purpose and a place within God's plan. To be persecuted for righteousness' sake is to be identified with Christ Himself, who endured the cross. The blessing is not merely future but present, as the kingdom is theirs even amid affliction. Their perseverance demonstrates a faith that is alive and powerful, inspiring hope and courage in the face of adversity.

When Jesus spoke these words, His listeners were drawn into a vision of life that transcended existing social and religious values. The Beatitudes turned upside down the expectations of greatness, power, and success, instead exalting the humble, the meek, the hungry for righteousness, and the persecuted. Each declaration pulses with warmth and vivid imagery, inviting readers not only to hear but to taste and feel the blessings within their own lives.

Imagine standing among the crowd on that mountaintop, faces illuminated by the morning sun, hearts stirred by these proclamations of grace. The listeners' eyes reveal glimpses of transformation, a weary soul brightening with hope, a hardened heart softening with conviction, a broken spirit buoyed by assurance. These blessings are more than words; they are divine invitations into a new way of being, shaped by mercy, purity, and peace.

Practically, the Beatitudes call forth a life lived counter to worldly ambition. They challenge believers to embrace humility in place of pride, to respond to sorrow with faith, to pursue righteousness above personal gain, and to extend mercy rather than judgment. Spiritually, they chart the contours of Christlike character, revealing the attitudes that make one fit for the kingdom of heaven.

Theologically, the Beatitudes offer a glimpse into the nature of God's reign, where the first shall be last and blessing flows to those who embody the gospel's radical love. They anticipate the fulfillment of all things when God's justice and peace will reign supreme, and His children will dwell with Him in unbroken fellowship. To meditate on these words is to stand at the threshold of heaven's mystery, invited to participate in the divine life themselves.

The poetic clarity of the Beatitudes continues to inspire and transform generations. Each statement, like a jewel set in a heavenly crown, reflects the light of God's promise. As radiant lanterns, they illuminate the pathways marked by grace and mercy, guiding the faithful toward the ultimate blessing: union with God and eternal joy in His kingdom.

In the silent echoes of this sermon, we find our own hearts drawn into the divine embrace. We are invited to mourn rightly, hunger deeply, show mercy boldly, and walk meekly, confident that these paths lead toward the blessedness that Jesus promises. The Beatitudes are more than teachings; they are windows into heaven itself, opening wide the gate to life renewed, hope restored, and love perfected.

New Law and Old: Fulfillment and Radical Grace

The mountain stood dressed in the golden hues of morning, a place where generations had lifted their voices in prayer and law. The air was still, heavy with the weight of centuries, of prophets, priests, and people who wrestled with God's commands written long ago on stone tablets, etched by the very hand that shaped the heavens and the earth. It was here, amid this hallowed quiet, that Jesus spoke, not simply to teach, but to unveil a radical truth, a light to pierce the shadows of tradition and legalism, revealing a new way that both honored and transcended what had come before.

In the earliest years of Israel's history, the Mosaic Law stood as the bedrock of covenantal relationship, a divine compass carved in commandments, statutes, and ordinances. These laws shaped the lives of the people, defining righteousness, justice, and holiness. From the Ten Commandments given amid thunder and fire on Mount Sinai to the numerous ritual codes and moral statutes, the Law was a complex tapestry that governed every facet of existence. It was a guide meant to weave the people's hearts into alignment with God's holy will. Yet, over time, the Law became a boundary fence, a record of "dos and don'ts," often rigid, external, and cold.

On that mountain so many ages later, Jesus stood poised to speak not merely as a teacher or rabbi, but as the fulfillment of that ancient law, the One who would bring law and grace into a profound harmony. His words breathed life into scripture and stirred the air like a fresh wind over parched earth, infusing the listeners with both awe and trembling anticipation. What He proclaimed was no mere revision or extension of the old code; it was a seismic spiritual shift that redefined the very essence of righteousness and called forth a deeper integrity from the soul's core.

Jesus began with a familiar phrase, "Ye have heard that it was said...", a deliberate invocation of the ancient commands, the echo of Mosaic authority. Yet, with each declaration, He peeled back layers of legalistic interpretation to reveal the heart beneath the letter. "But I say unto you..." became the clarion call of a new covenant, unveiling a law of the heart that beckoned not only obedience but transformation.

He spoke of anger and murder, revealing that true righteousness transcended the mere avoidance of physical violence. "Whosoever is angry with his brother without a cause shall be in danger of the judgment," He declared, uprooting the sin that festers beneath the surface of outward actions. The demand was not merely to withhold harm but to reconcile, to prevent the bitterness and estrangement that harden hearts and fracture the human community. What had been a command to "not kill" now dug deeper into the internal landscape of the soul.

Jesus turned to the commandment against adultery, extending its reach beyond physical acts to the inner realm of desire and thought. "Whosoever looked on a woman to lust after her hath committed adultery with her already in his heart." The standard of holiness was no longer external compliance but a pure heart, a radical call to holiness in thought as well as deed. In this revelation, the Law ceased to be a mere fence around behavior and became a mirror reflecting the intentions of the inner man.

He confronted divorce, teaching a permanence and sanctity to marriage exceeding common practice, challenging the cultural loopholes that allowed dissolution for trivial causes. This emphasized God's original design, unbreakable and divine, again shifting the focus from legal allowances to the covenantal integrity of the human heart.

On oaths, He urged a straightforwardness that made all vows unnecessary: "Let your communication be yea, yea; nay, nay." This simplicity echoed a trust in truthfulness that transcended elaborate religious rituals and legal phrasing.

Revenge was to be replaced by a grace that returns blessings for curses, a love that extends even to enemies, shattering cycles of retaliation. This teaching struck at the very roots of human nature, inviting a revolutionary ethic of mercy, patience, and generosity unheard of in worldly terms.

The command to "love your neighbor as yourself" was now expanded to "love your enemies," a love that would become the hallmark of Jesus's gospel, radical, unconditional, and costly.

Through these teachings, a new law emerged; one not carved in stone but written in flesh and spirit. Jesus was not abolishing the Law but fulfilling it, bringing it to its destined culmination in radical, living grace.

The Mosaic Law, with its detailed codes, found its perfect expression in a heart transformed by divine love.

The atmosphere on the mountaintop pulsed with tension and promise. The gathered crowd felt the electricity of a new dawn, as if the sun itself poured through the gathering clouds, scattering shadows that had long shrouded the soul. The call to righteousness was no longer a burdensome yoke but a pathway to true freedom, illuminated by the self-giving love of God manifest in the Son.

Jesus's words were seeds sown into the rugged soil of hearts steeped in tradition, yet hungry for renewal. These seeds would take root, grow, and someday yield a harvest that would transform the world. The difficult path of genuine holiness beckoned, demanding a shedding of old pretenses and superficial piety, calling instead for authenticity, mercy, and an inner purity that no mere law could command.

In this new teaching, righteousness became a dynamic force. It was no longer measured by outward conformity but by the condition of the heart and the quality of one's relationships, with God, with neighbor, with self. The values of humility, mercy, purity, peace, and love shaped this emergent kingdom ethic, the true fulfillment of the Law's deepest intention.

The imagery of light piercing shadow was not incidental. It symbolized the confrontation of divine truth with human darkness, the revelation of a higher righteousness that eclipses the old order. Like the dawn breaking over a long night, Jesus's words brought clarity and conviction, challenging the people to awaken to a new reality where God's grace met human need in the fullest measure.

The radical grace of Jesus's new law was not cheap or easy; it demanded a transformation of the whole person. It called for a surrender of pride, a renunciation of revenge, a willingness to forgive and love beyond natural inclinations. This grace was both gift and demand, offering a new possibility for life while requiring the costly obedience of faith.

Where Mosaic law had governed by rules and penalties, Jesus's teaching governed by invitation and power. The invitation was to live not by fear of condemnation but in the freedom of righteousness fulfilled by love, a love that renews, restores, and reconciles. The promise was that in embracing this law of the heart, believers would not only obey but experience the fullness of life God intended from the beginning of creation.

This was no mere religious reform or ethical refinement. It was the unveiling of the kingdom of God itself, a kingdom not of this world but breaking into it, bringing healing, hope, and new possibilities. Jesus's words on the mount formed the manifesto of this kingdom, the charter of a new humanity shaped by divine wisdom and mercy.

As listeners descended from the mount after that profound teaching, the impact lingered in the silence between words, the heavy pause of reflection and stirring challenge. Hearts were ignited, old certainties questioned, and a collective breath held in anticipation of what this new law might mean for lives, families, communities, and nations.

To truly grasp this movement from old to new, from law to grace, one must see beneath the surface of commandments to the deeper spiritual realities they sought to guard. The Law, given by Moses, was holy, just, and good, a perfect expression of God's will for His people. But it was incomplete, unable to change the human heart fully or bring about true righteousness. It acted as teacher and guide, pointing toward something greater.

Jesus, the fulfillment of the Law, entered human history to bring that greater reality. His teaching on the mount stands as a pivotal moment where the fullness of the Law is revealed in the light of Divine love poured into human hearts.

The spiritual shift is massive: from external compliance to internal transformation; from judgment to mercy; from limitation to liberation; from resentment to gracious love. This shift does not discard the Old but completes and perfects it, revealing that at the heart of God's law is the loving character He desires to form in His people.

In the years and centuries that followed, the tension between the Old Law and the New remains a profound theme within the Christian experience. Many struggled to understand how one could be both faithful to scripture and embrace the overflowing grace of Christ's teaching. Yet, the mountain's message remains clear: true righteousness is a matter of the heart, empowered by the Spirit and lived out in love.

The "New Law and Old" is not a conflict but a harmonious symphony of divine purpose, law fulfilled in grace, justice completed in mercy, holiness expressed through love. It is the tension of the cross where justice and grace meet, where human sin is met with divine forgiveness. It is the ever-unfolding mystery of redemption that will continue to transform souls until that day when every knee shall bow, and every tongue confess that Jesus Christ is Lord, to the glory of God the Father.

As readers journey through this foundational teaching, they are invited to reflect on their own hearts, on the shadows that linger and the light that calls forth new life. The mountain's challenge is one of radical honesty and hopeful courage, beckoning all to step beyond the familiar and enter the expansive realm of God's grace made manifest in the life and words of Jesus Christ.

Here, in the interplay between the old and the new, is the Christ who fulfills the Law, the Light that conquers darkness, and the Seed of change planted deep within the soil of human history, destined to grow, flourish, and bear eternal fruit.

Miracles of Light and Hope

Turning Water into Wine: Joy's First Sign

The day at Cana of Galilee unfolded with all the warmth and vibrancy of a village gathered in celebration. The air was thick with the mingling scents of fresh earth, crushed grapevines, and spiced food, as friends and kin rejoiced in the union of two hearts. Laughter wove through the crowds, mingling with the soft murmur of conversation and the occasional joyous shout from children running between stalls. Sunlight filtered gently through leaves heavy with the season's ripened fruit, casting dappled light upon the faces of those gathered. This was no ordinary day, yet those present had no inkling that before the feast's end, they would witness an event that carried the tender promise of renewal far beyond the bounds of this earthly celebration.

The wedding was an occasion marked by old customs, echoing through generations, the breaking of bread, the sharing of wine, the intertwining of families. The aroma of freshly baked bread interlaced with the sweet, floral notes of crushed grape must wafted from barrels tucked beneath the tables. The taste of the evening itself was alive in every bite and sip: warm loaves softened under olive oil, tender lamb slow-roasted with herbs, and the rich, honeyed wine that drew smiles across parched lips.

Yet as the guests reveled, a subtle shadow began to fall over the day's joy, the wine, the symbol of celebration and life, was running low. In the culture of the time, wine was not simply a drink but an embodiment of festivity, hospitality, and blessing. Its absence threatened not just the party's continuation, but the honor of the hosts. Such an omission could bring embarrassment amid a gathering that valued generosity and abundance.

It was within this moment of growing concern that Jesus' presence quietly began to assert itself amid the unfolding scene. His mother, Mary, aware of the impending lack, approached Him with a confidence born of intimate knowledge. Though Jesus spoke gently, "Mine hour is not yet come", Mary's understanding and faith were unmistakable. Her words to the servants were simple but profound: "Whatsoever he saith unto you, do it."

The servants obeyed without hesitation, their hands dipping to fill the empty vessels with water drawn from the stone jars designated for ceremonial purification. These jars, each holding twenty to thirty gallons, were typically filled for the fasting rituals that marked purity before meals or worship. Yet now, they stood ready to witness a transformation that would forever meld earthly custom and divine intervention.

The water filled the jars slowly, the clear liquid shimmering beneath the golden light of the evening sun. There was a stillness as all eyes turned to Jesus, who then instructed the servants to draw from the newly filled vessels and take the water to the master of the feast. Expectation hung in the air, mingling with a sense of hushed anticipation. When the first taste touched the master's lips, surprise blossomed across his face, an illumination of wonder breaking through his composed countenance.

"This beginning of miracles did Jesus in Cana of Galilee," John the Evangelist recounts, "and manifested forth his glory; and his disciples believed on him." The water had been changed into wine, a transformation not just of substance but of meaning and promise. It was a miracle of abundance, signaling an overflow of joy and the presence of a glory that surpassed human understanding.

This newly created wine was described as being of the finest quality, "better than that which the guests had first tasted." The contrast was striking: when the celebration began, the ordinary wine had been sufficient, but now, in this sign of grace and plenitude, the best was reserved for the latter part of the feast. The guests, unaware of the source, savored the rich depth and smoothness of this new wine, their senses enraptured by its fullness and brightness. In that moment, taste became a testament to the divine, and the texture spoke of a perfect blending between earth and heaven.

The miracle's effect rippled quietly yet powerfully through those present. It did not demand their immediate belief, nor did it overwhelm with spectacle, but rather gently invited them into hope, hope that the ordinary could be transformed, that joy could be expanded beyond measure, and that the hand of God moved tenderly through the fabric of everyday life. The wedding guests would remember the sweetness of that wine, the unexpected richness that lingered on the tongue long after the feast had ended.

It is in this mingling of earthly festivity and heavenly intervention that the first sign of Jesus' public ministry reveals itself. The wedding at Cana was not merely an isolated moment of wonder but a revelation that the kingdom of God was near, a kingdom marked by overflowing grace, celebration, and the transforming power of divine love.

The sensory fullness of that day, the sight of pressed vines, the tangible warmth of clay jars, the aroma of fermenting grapes, the sound of laughter echoing over tilled fields, all combined within the miracle to awaken a deeper awareness. The miracle at Cana invited all who witnessed it to believe in a God who delights in human joy, who cares for the small details of life, and who calls His children into a new covenant of hope and abundance.

From the quiet filling of water jars to the first sip that ignited surprise and delight, the story holds a powerful lesson about transformation. Water, a symbol of purification and life's simplest necessity, became wine, a symbol of celebration, covenant, and divine blessing. It speaks to the miraculous potential in everyday moments and the hope that can blossom when discerned through faith. In this act, Jesus showed that His mission would bring not only judgment or sacrifice but restoration and the overflowing joy of salvation.

The lasting impression of Cana is one of joy rekindled, not just in wine, but in the human spirit, beckoning believers into a lived experience where grace is manifest in the tangible, the ordinary becomes extraordinary, and hope is renewed in the presence of the divine. It stands as a beacon in the ministry of Christ, shining a light on the nature of His work: to transform, to heal, to bring abundance, and to invite all into the celebration of life under God.

As the feast at Cana drew to a close, the witnesses carried with them more than the memory of sumptuous food and fine wine. They carried the undeniable echo of a moment when heaven touched earth, a whisper that the kingdom of God was being unveiled in myriad quiet signs, beginning with a simple yet profound act of love shown in turning water into wine. This miracle marked the dawn of a ministry that would gather people from all walks of life into a new covenant of hope, promise, and joy eternal.

Healing the Blind and the Deaf: Opening New Worlds

In the days when Jesus walked among the people of Israel, the common reality of suffering and limitation weighed heavily upon many. Among the most profound afflictions were those that robbed men and women of their senses, the gift of sight and the faculty of hearing. To live in a world veiled by darkness or muted by silence was to exist at the margins, separated from the fullness of life and communion with others. Into this somber reality, Jesus brought a light that pierced the deepest shadows, opening new worlds for those long entombed in physical and spiritual blindness and deafness.

One such scene unfolds beside the bustling roads and dusty byways where Jesus traveled. The air hangs thick with anticipation as the crowds gather, drawn by whispers and rumors of astonishing healings. Among the onlookers are those burdened by their own infirmities, their hearts flickering with hope amid a sea of doubt. A man, blind from birth, sits quietly, untouched by the vibrant colors of the marketplace, the radiance of the morning sun never painting his world. His eyes, once thought empty, hold a silent yearning instead.

Jesus approaches, the murmurs rising into a hush. Kneeling beside the blind man, He takes the dust of the earth into His hands and, with deliberate care, touches the closed eyes. Then, with a voice both gentle and authoritative, He commands, "Receive thy sight." In that instant, the man's eyelids flutter, and the darkness begins to dissipate, replaced first by shapes, then by the subtle gradations of light and shadow, and finally by the dazzling tableau of colors bursting forth like a new creation.

The crowd gasps, the sound a chorus of astonishment and praise. The man himself is overwhelmed, his hands trembling as they reach up to touch the contours of a world newly alive to him. The rich hues of the sky, the green leaves fluttering in the breeze, the faces gleaming with joy, all flood his senses. His transformation is more than physical; it is the birth of a new identity, a restoration to the community from which he had long been alienated. Tears stream down his face, mixing with smiles of disbelief and laughter that ring pure and free.

Nearby, another miracle stirs, this time wrought upon a man deaf and almost mute from a birth defect. His world is a still silence, cut off from the melodies of birdsong and the whispered kindness of those who love him. Yet here, standing before the crowd, Jesus lays His hands upon the man's ears and his tongue, gently pressing and whispering words of restoration. Suddenly, the man's ears unlock to the fullness of sound, the murmur of the crowd, the voice of Jesus, the cry of children at play.

Then, as if freed from chains, his tongue loosens, and for the first time words, not just sounds, but words filled with meaning, begin to form. Shouts of amazement rise up, echoing across the hills and streets. The man's face glows with newfound confidence, his speech now a bridge connecting him with others, opening avenues of relationship and belonging that had been closed. His joy is infectious, enveloping all who witness this touch of divine grace.

Throughout these healings, those who stand nearby embody a mixture of skepticism and wonder. Some murmur doubts, questioning if such acts can be from God or are mere trickery. Others fall silent, awestruck by the undeniable power at work. The contrast is vivid: the blindness of disbelief versus the illuminated faith kindled in hearts by the spectacle of transformation. In these moments, light does not merely brighten the eyes of the healed but pierces the darkness that shrouds human understanding and openness to the divine.

This interplay of light and darkness permeates every detail. Before healing, the blind man's world is painted in grays and shadows; the deaf man's existence is muted, lacking the vibrant chorus of sound. After Jesus' touch, these sensory realms explode into brilliance, the once blind man sees the radiant gold of wheat fields and the deep blue of the evening sky; the once deaf man marvels at the crispness of footsteps approaching and the gentle murmur of prayer.

Yet the miracle extends beyond sense perception alone. It is a profound opening of new realities. To regain sight or hearing is not simply to restore what was lost; it is to receive a transformed existence marked by hope, dignity, and the flourishing of human potential. The healed individuals now participate fully in the sacred dance of life, no longer spectators on the margins but active, vibrant members of their communities. Their identities are renewed and reframed in the light of divine healing.

The narrative also carefully traces the emotional journey of those healed. Initially, they carry the weight of isolation and despair, shadows cast not only by their physical conditions but also by years of marginalization and rejection. The moment their senses reawaken, they experience a cascade of emotions: bewilderment at the flood of sensations, gratitude to the One who restored them, and a swelling joy tempered by humility. This emotional depth grounds the miraculous in authentic human experience, bridging the divine and the earthly.

For the onlookers, the bold act of healing challenges their own perceptions. Witnessing the blind see, and the deaf hear, confronts them with the tangible presence of God moving in their midst. Faith, once theoretical or distant, becomes real and urgent. Some hearts harden further, their doubts growing as they wrestle with explanations and consequences; others incline toward belief, drawn irresistibly to the light that defies darkness.

In these encounters, Jesus reveals more than physical restoration, He reveals the heart of God's kingdom, where light and life overcome the shadows of this fallen world. The biblical accounts, rich in imagery and emotion, convey the profound significance of these moments. The healed do not simply receive a cure; they enter into a new covenant of existence marked by spiritual awakening and divine favor.

Metaphorically, the healing of the blind and the deaf speaks to every soul longing for clarity and understanding, for the ability to perceive God's truth and hear His voice. It is an invitation not only to physical wholeness but also to spiritual illumination. The acts of Jesus break through darkness, both seen and unseen, offering all who witness and believe a hope that transcends mere survival, promising abundant life eternally.

Thus, the narratives of healing unfold as vibrant tapestries woven with light piercing darkness. They position Jesus as the divine agent of restoration, the path from limitation to freedom, from despair to joy.

Each miracle is a revelation that God's kingdom is at hand, manifesting in the simple yet profound opening of eyes and ears to a broader, richer existence. For those healed, for the witnesses, and for the generations to come, these moments resonate as eternal testimony to the power of divine love to open new worlds where once there was only darkness and silence.

Calming the Storm: Peace Amid Chaos

The lake was restless, its surface whipped into frothing waves by a furious wind that howled and shrieked across the open water. The wooden boat, small and fragile amid the vast tempest, was tossed from crest to trough like a leaf caught in a storm. Thick sheets of spray whipped into the faces of the disciples, blurring vision and chilling skin with the cold touch of the storm's breath. The roar of thunder crashed overhead, and lightning cracked briefly, illuminating the tumultuous sea in stark, ghostly flashes. Fear gripped the hearts of the men, seasoned fishermen though many were, for nature's fury had become an overwhelming force beyond human control.

In the midst of this chaos sat Jesus, serene and composed, reclining on a cushion in the stern. His eyes remained closed, his body unshaken by the violence of the storm that raged all around Him. The contrast between the divine stillness within and the frantic thrashing without was palpable. The disciples, wracked with desperation, scrambled about the boat, battening down loose lines and trying desperately to keep water from flooding the hull. Their shouts mingled with the thunder, drowned out by the persistent roar of the wind and the slap of waves against wood.

The tempest was more than a natural phenomenon; it was a living force that pressed upon the vulnerable boat with an unforgiving weight. The vessel creaked and groaned, threatening to break apart beneath the swell. Each man was acutely aware of his own helplessness, the thin line between survival and disaster stretched taut beneath the shrieking sky. Their faith was tested amid the raging elements that seemed intent on swallowing them whole.

It was in this crucible of fear and doubt that Jesus rose from His place of calm. He stood, tall and commanding, silhouetted against the darkened horizon. His voice, when He spoke, was the embodiment of calm authority, cutting through the cacophony with a power that was both gentle and irresistible. "Peace, be still," He said.

The effect was immediate and profound. The wind ceased its howling, as if it had been commanded into silence. The waves, tall and menacing moments before, stalled in mid-motion and then receded, the lake's surface smoothing to a mirror-like calm. A stillness fell, deep and complete, enveloping the boat like a protective cloak. The disciples looked about them, wide-eyed and speechless, each wrestling with the sudden cessation of terror and the overwhelming peace that followed.

This moment, preserved within the sacred pages of the King James Bible, is not merely a recounting of a miraculous event, it is a profound tableau of faith and divine power. The storm, vicious and consuming, becomes an emblem of the trials and fears that beset every human soul. The turbulent waves reflect the inner turmoil experienced in the face of adversity, when all seems lost and hope is fleeting. Yet the command of Jesus reveals a higher truth: amid the fiercest chaos, divine peace reigns supreme.

The sensory drama of this event draws believers into the heart of the narrative. The roar of the winds, the spray that lashes painfully, the trembling wood beneath trembling feet, all serve to magnify the emotional intensity. Readers can feel the cold sting of the spray and hear the relentless pounding of waves, as though standing within the storm themselves. The physicality of the scene makes the sudden stillness all the more piercing. In stark contrast, the quiet is not empty but vibrant with the presence of calm assurance.

Spiritually, the calm that follows the tempest speaks to the victory of faith over fear. The disciples' initial panic reflects our own human tendency to succumb to dread when confronted by life's insurmountable challenges. Yet the presence of Christ brings not merely safety but a profound peace that transcends circumstance. His words "Peace, be still" echo as a timeless command not just to nature but to the soul unsettled by worry and anguish.

This miracle carries rich symbolic meaning. The storm can be seen as the world's opposition to God's kingdom, a manifestation of the disorder and turmoil that come with living in a fallen world. The boat, vulnerable and small, represents the Church or the individual believer navigating the perilous seas of life. Jesus' mastery over the wind and waves affirms His sovereignty over creation and His power to bring order from chaos. In this way, the episode reassures the faithful that no storm, whether physical, emotional, or spiritual, is beyond His control.

Moreover, the sudden silence of the lake is a metaphor for the transformative power of divine intervention. Where there was fear, peace; where there was destruction, safety; where there was dark uncertainty, light and clarity. The masterful command issued with quiet authority is a testament to the nature of Jesus' power, not violent or forced, but sovereign, gentle, and deliberate. The miracle invites believers to entrust their fears to Him, confident that His command can bring calm to any storm.

The disciples' response also provides a window into the human encounter with the divine. Following the miracle, they marveled and asked among themselves, "What manner of man is this, that even the winds and the sea obey him?" Their awe is a recognition of the mystery and power of Jesus' identity. For readers, their astonishment serves as an invitation to deepen faith, to acknowledge that Jesus is no mere teacher or prophet, but the Son of God, Lord over all creation.

This episode, recorded in the gospels of Mark as well as Matthew and Luke, is a singular moment that captures multiple layers of meaning. Its immediacy and drama convey the reality of the miracle, while the rich symbolism points beyond to eternal spiritual truths. Here is a narrative that speaks across centuries, inviting every generation to consider the storms in their own lives and the power of faith to still the waves.

In contemplating this passage, one cannot help but reflect on the broader context of Jesus' ministry. Throughout His time on earth, He consistently demonstrated authority, not only over sickness and sin but also over the natural world. Each miracle underscored His divine station and His mission to bring salvation and peace to a troubled humanity. The Calming of the Storm stands out because it confronts a universal fear: the fear of death, destruction, and being overwhelmed by forces beyond comprehension.

The lake, most scholars agree, is the Sea of Galilee, a famously storm-prone body of water enclosed by hills that can channel sudden gusts and furious tempests. The disciples knew its volatility well, having weathered many storms before. Their fear here speaks not only to the ferocity of the storm but also to the unexpectedness of the danger, when a storm's fury catches even the most seasoned off guard. This amplifies the impact of Jesus' serene authority amid panic.

The narrative's emphasis on Jesus resting peacefully highlights a deep spiritual truth: for the believer, faith in Christ allows for rest amid trials. The juxtaposition of divine peace and human alarm calls readers to a higher standard of trust, to rely not on their own strength but on the sovereign power of the Savior. This lesson remains poignant and practical for modern readers navigating their own tempests of doubt, loss, and fear.

The disciples' transition from panic to amazement also offers a model for the believer's journey. The storm serves as a trial, faith as the anchor, and Jesus' intervention as the deliverance. By witnessing the miracle, the disciples grow in understanding and trust, a trajectory that mirrors every Christian's path from uncertainty to conviction. The power that calms the sea speaks likewise to the power that calms the heart, inviting a spiritual stillness beneath life's storms.

The words "Peace, be still" are evocative beyond their immediate narrative purpose. They have become a spiritual invocation for centuries of believers seeking refuge from anxiety and fear. These words express the essence of the gospel message: that Christ brings peace not as the world gives, but as the world cannot understand. The tranquility He bestows is not dependent on circumstances but flows from His sovereign will and care.

In the realm of biblical symbolism, water often represents chaos and danger, a force that threatens life and order. Throughout scripture, God's authority is shown in His dominion over the waters, from the creation narrative in Genesis to the Exodus, where the Red Sea parts at His command. The calming of the sea by Jesus is the continuation of this divine theme, a dramatic demonstration that the God revealed in Christ has power over the primal forces that threaten human existence.

Examining the metaphorical depth of the episode, the storm can also symbolize internal conflict, the swelling fears, doubts, and emotional tempests that buffet the human spirit. The shaking boat becomes the fragile human psyche vulnerable to despair. Jesus' command represents the healing and ordering of internal chaos, the restoration of peace amid mental and spiritual upheaval. For readers, this spiritual emblem aligns with the experience of being comforted and steadied by faith in turbulent times.

Furthermore, the scene encapsulates the relationship between divinity and humanity. The disciples' vulnerability and fear contrast sharply with Jesus' calm assurance. Yet, He is present physically among them, sharing in their peril but not overwhelmed by it. This intimacy reveals a God who enters human suffering, not as a distant observer, but as a powerful redeemer who brings peace from the heart of trial and tribulation.

The lesson extends beyond the literal storm. Every believer faces storms unique to their own lives, loss, uncertainty, sickness, betrayal, and spiritual dryness. The story of Jesus calming the sea becomes a touchstone for hope: no storm can ultimately defeat the faithful who call upon His name. His sovereign peace is available to still the roiling waves of fear and despair.

The narrative also serves to instruct about the nature of faith. When the storm threatens, the disciples are terrified; but after the miracle, they begin to grasp the identity of their Master more clearly. Faith is not merely a passive belief but an active trust in the character and power of Christ. It invites the believer to confront fear honestly while choosing to rest in the assurance of God's control.

Throughout the gospel accounts, Jesus forms a comprehensive image of the Messiah who heals, teaches, and commands. The miracle of calming the storm is a vivid pageant of His authority over all things. It invites meditation on the sovereignty of God in a world that often seems riddled with chaos and uncertainty. The peace He grants is the foundation upon which faith is built, a peace that neither time nor tempest can undo.

In contemplating this event, one may also reflect on the careful literary craft of the gospel writers. Their vivid use of sensory detail, the choking spray, the splintering timbers, the shrieking cries of the wind, immerses the reader fully into the scene. This heightens the tension, makes the crisis palpable, and prepares the heart for the release into profound calm. The narrative's balance of drama and serenity echoes the spiritual journey from turmoil into refuge.

The enduring power of this story is found in its invitation: to experience the reality of Jesus' peace. For those who have faced tempests in life, the image of the Savior standing calmly and commanding the elements offers reassurance. It suggests that amid the most violent storms, an abiding peace is possible, one rooted not in human circumstances but in the divine presence.

Ultimately, the calming of the storm transcends the specific moment on the Sea of Galilee. It becomes a living metaphor for the transformative power of faith and the presence of God in the middle of life's chaotic moments. The storm-tossed sea is not the end but a stage upon which the grandeur of divine peace is revealed, and human hearts are called to awaken to the mastery of the One who commands the winds and waves with gentle authority.

Thus, the miracle speaks to every believer, the weary, the fearful, the doubting, to receive the peace that Jesus offers. To trust in His power and grace, even when the world around swells with uncertainty and danger. It reassures that no matter how wild the storm, the voice of divine calm can silence it, restoring hope and courage to the soul.

In that sublime moment, when the waters ceased their wrath and the wind was stilled, the disciples glimpsed the heart of the kingdom of God: a kingdom where fear is conquered by faith, chaos subdued by order, and human frailty met with infinite strength. Here lies the profound spiritual emblem of peace amid chaos, an everlasting testament to the mastery of divine power in human trials, a beacon of light for all who journey through life's storms.

Raising the Dead: Triumph Over Finality

In the quiet village of Bethany, a profound sorrow had settled upon the hearts of all who knew him. Lazarus, beloved brother to Mary and Martha, had succumbed to death's final embrace. Four days had passed since his breath ceased, since the stillness of the tomb swallowed him whole. The air hung heavy with grief, mourning whispers filled the homes, and the once vibrant life that Lazarus had been was now only a memory etched in tears. It is into this deep shadow of loss and despair that Jesus came, a presence that would soon rewrite the narrative of death itself.

The story begins with Mary and Martha sending word to Jesus: "Lord, behold, he whom thou lovest is sick." The urgency of this message, so simple yet so profound, rings with human vulnerability and faith. Even as Jesus hears this plea, there is a stillness to His response, a measured calm that belies the storm of emotions surrounding this tragedy. "This sickness is not unto death, but for the glory of God, that the Son of God might be glorified thereby," He declares. These words, pregnant with divine purpose, prepare us for a miracle that transcends ordinary understanding.

Jesus delays His journey, arriving in Bethany only after Lazarus's death. The scene that unfolds is thick with mourning; the air is heavy with weeping, lamentations, and the oppressive presence of death. Martha meets Jesus first, confessing her grief yet expressing unwavering belief: "If thou hadst been here, my brother had not died. But I know that even now, whatsoever thou wilt ask of God, God will give it thee." Her faith punctuates the mourning, piercing through the sorrow like a beacon. Jesus responds, "Thy brother shall rise again," planting a seed of hope amidst the desolation.

When Mary arrives and falls at Jesus's feet, her grief becomes overwhelming. Seeing her weeping, Jesus is "deeply moved in spirit, and grieveth," revealing the profound compassion of the Savior. His own tears mingle with those of His friends, demonstrating that even the Son of God was touched by the shadow of death's pain. This moment of shared sorrow humanizes the divine, drawing us into an intimate relationship with Jesus, One who understands our anguish yet wields power beyond it.

The procession to the tomb is heavy with solemnity. The rock-sealed grave represents the irreversible finality of death, a boundary that no ordinary mortal can cross. Yet Jesus commands it to be opened, His voice resounding with authority: "Lazarus, come forth." What follows is a moment charged with tension so thick it could be cut with a knife. The crowd holds its breath; the silence itself speaks. Then, as the stone rolls away, the sight of Lazarus, alive and restored, emerges from the darkness of the tomb, bound still in graveclothes, yet breathing the breath of life once more.

This miracle defies natural law and strikes at the very heart of human fear: death. The triumph over this finality is not only physical but deeply symbolic. It is a foreshadowing of the ultimate victory that Jesus would claim over death on the cross and through His own resurrection. The restoration of Lazarus serves as an embodiment of hope, the promise that death is not the end, but a transition into a new life held in God's loving hands.

The sensory imagery surrounding this event crystallizes the transformation from despair to joy. Shadows that once weighed down the spirit recede as dawn's first light breaks upon Bethany. The chill of the tomb gives way to the warmth of living presence; cold stone is replaced by the warmth of flesh and pulse. The mourners' loud lamentations turn into cries of wonder and exultation. The air, once heavy with the scent of death, is filled now with the fragrant breath of life renewed.

Through this miracle, themes of hope and restoration intertwine with divine love in a tapestry that speaks to the very core of human existence. The raising of Lazarus is more than a miraculous event; it is a revelation of God's heart toward His creation. It proclaims loud and clear that love does not end in death, that darkness will ultimately yield to light, and that the God who commands life is unyielding in His compassion and power.

Moreover, the narrative holds a wider spiritual significance. It calls believers into a deeper trust in the promises of Christ, encouraging them to see beyond the pain of loss to the future resurrection assured in Him. The miracle sets a pattern for all who struggle under the shadow of death's sting: a divine pledge that life, in its ultimate and eternal form, transcends the grave. It assures that death is but a passage, not a permanent exile.

The air of awe that enveloped the crowd as Lazarus emerged foreshadowed the powerful change Jesus was bringing to the world, an unveiling of God's kingdom where death would be swallowed up in victory. The tension, grief, and desperate hope of those present all blend into a moment frozen in sacred mystery, inviting us to witness the divine triumph that undergirds all Christian faith.

The subsequent days after Lazarus's resurrection ripple through the lives of many, touching not only the immediate circle of friends but also stirring the hearts of skeptical onlookers, the Pharisees, and the disciples alike. This miraculous act became a turning point, both a sign of Jesus's divine authority and a provocation that hastened the course toward the Passion. Yet, in this calling back from the dead, we glimpse the full scope of Jesus's mission: to bring life where there is death, hope where there is despair, and light where there is darkness.

The raising of Lazarus invites each reader to stand at the border between death and life, to look into the tombs of personal grief and loss, and to hear the call of Jesus to "come forth." It challenges hearts to reckon with the sacred mystery of life's transcendence, where mortality is overcome by the everlasting love of God. In this way, the miracle remains eternally vibrant, a testament that death does not have the final word, and that through Christ, the dawn always follows the night.

The story of Lazarus is one chapter among several in the grand narrative of Jesus's miracles, yet its potency is unmatched because it touches upon the most profound existential question: Is there hope beyond death? Through the interplay of faith, divine power, and human response, it answers with a resolute and radiant "Yes." This miracle speaks not only to those who witnessed it long ago but to the soul of every believer walking through the shadows of this world toward the promise of eternal dawn.

In reflecting on this event, it is impossible not to be enveloped by a profound sense of the sacred mystery. The tomb, once a symbol of finality and silence, becomes a place where the breath of God moves mightily, breaking the chains of death. The raising of Lazarus transcends a simple miracle; it emerges as an eternal testament to God's sovereignty over life and death and His endless capacity to restore and renew. It calls us to marvel, to hope, and to place our trust in the love that animates all creation.

This narrative also encourages contemplation of the tension between the seen and unseen, the temporal and eternal, the bones and dust that the tomb holds, and the life that God can breathe back into them. It is in this tension that faith grows strong. To believe in Jesus's power to raise the dead is to believe in His ultimate authority over all things, and to recognize that His love reaches beyond the limits of human understanding.

Ultimately, the raising of Lazarus paints a portrait of Jesus as the source of life itself. It brings into sharp focus the reality that while death touches every human life, it does not triumph over those who are united with Christ. Through this miracle, readers stand on holy ground where earthly sorrows meet heavenly glory; they hear the voice that calls forth life from death and witness divine love made manifest.

As the shadows vanished in Bethany, so they vanish in every heart that embraces the truth of Jesus's resurrection power. The story of Lazarus is a clarion call to hope, a vivid reminder that in Christ, death is not an end but a beginning, a passage into eternal light. It reassures that no matter how deep the darkness, the dawn of God's love breaks through, making all things new.

In the echo of this miracle, the Christian faith finds its cornerstone. The raising of the dead is not only a testament to Jesus's divine authority but also a profound symbol of the promise given to all who believe: the promise of resurrection, renewal, and everlasting life. This is the triumph over finality, the victory of light over darkness, life over death, and hope over despair. In the face of death's shadow, Jesus shines forth as the living hope, the resurrection and the life, embracing all with the assurance that through Him, death is conquered and eternal life is granted.

Thus, in the rich tapestry of miracles that illuminate Jesus's ministry, the raising of Lazarus stands as a pinnacle of divine intervention. It teaches that God's love refuses to accept death as the ultimate end, that hope remains alive beyond the grave, and that faith in Christ holds the power to overcome even the darkest and most final of human realities. The sacred mystery unveiled in this story invites all to step beyond fear and mourning, to enter into the dawn of resurrection joy, and to live in the light of God's eternal promise.

Friendships and Fables

The Twelve Disciples: Bonds of Faith and Flaws

In the tapestry of Jesus Christ's earthly ministry, the twelve disciples stand as the closest companions to the Son of God, a band of men whose lives would forever intertwine with the greatest story ever told. These twelve were not extraordinary by human standards; they bore the marks of common life, ordinary fishermen, a tax collector, men with dreams, doubts, fears, and frailties. Yet, through their encounters with Jesus, they were transformed, bonded by faith and forged in the fires of trial and revelation. This subchapter delves into the vivid portraits of these twelve men, exploring their personalities, struggles, and the spiritual metamorphosis they underwent. It seeks to reveal their humanity alongside their chosenness, inviting readers into the warmth, complexity, and raw honesty of their journey with Christ.

From the beginning, we meet Simon Peter, a figure simultaneously bold and impulsive, whose heart was fierce and who walked a path marked by both great faith and human weakness. Peter, a fisherman by trade, carried the hopes of leadership among the group. Jesus called him, ceasing his work with the nets, saying, "Follow me, and I will make you fishers of men" (Matthew 4:19). Peter's impetuous nature was evident when he first confessed Jesus as the Christ, declaring, "Thou art the Christ, the Son of the living God" (Matthew 16:16). This admission was pivotal, a moment signaling his recognition of Jesus's divine mission. Yet, Peter's impulsiveness also led to moments of doubt and fear, including his infamous denial of Christ on the night of His arrest (Matthew 26:69-75). Despite these failures, Peter's story is one of restoration and unwavering devotion. Jesus's forgiveness and commission to "feed my sheep" (John 21:17) reveal a disciple deeply human yet profoundly redeemed.

Alongside Peter stood his brother Andrew, whose role is often quieter but no less vital. Andrew was the first disciple called, a disciple who immediately sought others, bringing his brother Peter to Jesus (John 1:40-42). His faithful heart shines through his eagerness to share the Good News, reflecting a disciple who understood the value of community and witnessing. More reserved than Peter, Andrew nonetheless embodied the disciple's calling to lead others to Christ gently and persistently.

James and John, sons of Zebedee, present a complex picture of ambition, passion, and learning humility. Known as the "sons of thunder" (Mark 3:17), their zeal was evident in their desire for prominence in the coming kingdom. This ambition once stirred resentment when they requested seats of honor beside Jesus in His glory (Mark 10:35-37). Yet, through their intimate moments with Christ, they grasped lessons in servant leadership and sacrifice. John, the beloved disciple, is noted for his closeness to Jesus, often leaning on the Master's breast at the Last Supper (John 13:23). James, the elder, would eventually become a martyred leader in the early church, a testament to the fiery devotion sparked by Christ's call.

Philip and Bartholomew (also identified as Nathanael) exemplify humility and the recognition of truth. Philip's simple faith is seen as he brings others to Jesus, including Nathanael, whom Jesus described as "an Israelite indeed, in whom is no guile" (John 1:47). Their stories are imbued with moments of revelation and amazement, such as Nathanael's declaration upon meeting Jesus, "Rabbi, thou art the Son of God; thou art the King of Israel" (John 1:49). Yet, even these men were not perfect, as seen when Philip struggles to understand Jesus's teachings fully, urging Him to show the Father (John 14:8–9), illustrating a yearning for clarity amidst mystery.

Thomas, often remembered as "Doubting Thomas," embodies the human struggle with faith and the desire for tangible evidence. After

Jesus's resurrection, Thomas expressed his disbelief, famously requiring to see and touch Jesus's wounds before believing (John 20:24-29). This response reveals the authentic human tension between skepticism and faith. Yet, Thomas's moment of confession, "My Lord and my God," stands as a profound declaration of his ultimate belief, demonstrating faith forged through questioning and encounter rather than blind acceptance.

Matthew, the tax collector, offers a striking contrast to his fellow disciples. Often scorned by Jews for his profession, he left behind a life of perceived corruption to follow Jesus (Matthew 9:9). Matthew's transformation reflects the radical inclusivity of Jesus's call, the invitation extended to the outcast and sinner. His meticulous recording of Jesus's teachings, in the Gospel of Matthew, serves as a lasting testament to the personal encounter that redefined his life's purpose, from collecting earthly wealth to investing in heavenly treasure.

James, son of Alphaeus, and Thaddaeus (also called Judas, son of James) remain somewhat shadowed figures, their personalities less defined in Scripture but equally part of the inner circle. Their presence reminds readers of the often unsung roles within a community of faith, men who faithfully followed and supported the mission, contributing quietly but steadfastly. These disciples embody the silent endurance and perseverance required in the journey of faith.

Simon the Zealot adds a dimension of political and social passion to the group. As a member of the Zealots, a revolutionary movement seeking Jewish liberation, his decision to follow Jesus indicates a radical reorientation of zeal, from earthly rebellion to spiritual transformation. Simon's story underscores the diversity within the discipleship, the meeting of varied backgrounds unified in a common mission. His journey symbolizes the call to channel fervor into faithful service.

Finally, Judas Iscariot presents a troubling yet essential figure. Chosen among the twelve, yet betrayer of the Lord, Judas's story is a cautionary tale of misplaced priorities and the peril of greed. His role as treasurer and his eventual betrayal for thirty pieces of silver (Matthew 26:14-16) reveals the tension between human weakness and divine sovereignty. Judas's tragic end, his remorse and death (Matthew 27:3-5), echoes the profound consequences of choosing earthly gain over loyalty to the Savior. In Judas, we see the stark contrast to the other disciples, reminding readers of the persistent possibility of failure even within the closest circles of faith.

Beyond their individual stories, the twelve formed a tightly knit fellowship marked by shared experiences and collective growth. Their time with Jesus was shaped by moments of teaching, witnessing miracles, and enduring persecution. They traveled together, ate together, argued, and learned, bound not only by proximity but by the growing revelation of who Jesus was. The moments recorded in Scripture reveal human interactions laden with both warmth and tension, such as the dispute among the disciples over who was the greatest (Luke 22:24-27), pointing to ongoing struggles with pride even in the presence of holiness.

Their doubts and fears were ever-present. When storms threatened their boat, their cry was often one of panic rather than faith (Mark 4:35-41). When Jesus foretold suffering and death, their understanding faltered, revealing the gap between expectation and divine purpose (Mark 8:31-33). Yet, each trial was an opportunity for growth, a deepening of trust in the One who called them beyond themselves.

The relational dynamics among the disciples illustrate the complexity of human friendship intertwined with divine mission. Peter's leadership was sometimes challenged by the more contemplative John or the practical Thomas. The ambitions of James and John met the humility of Philip and Bartholomew. The quiet faithfulness of lesser-known disciples stood alongside the bold declarations of Peter and Judas's betrayal. This mosaic of personalities reflects the church's makeup, a community of varied temperaments unified by faith in Christ.

Together, these men witnessed the fullness of Jesus's ministry, from miraculous healings to piercing parables, from the Mount of Transfiguration to the Garden of Gethsemane. They beheld His compassion, strength, and submission to the Father's will. Their transformation was not instantaneous but gradual, marked by stumbling steps and growing confidence.

After Jesus's resurrection, the disciples were forever altered. The same men who once fled in fear became bold proclaimers of the gospel. Peter stood before crowds at Pentecost, unafraid to declare the risen Christ (Acts 2). Thomas, having touched the wounds of Jesus, spread the message of resurrection beyond Jerusalem. Even Simon the Zealot took the faith to new lands, and James's martyrdom cemented the cost of discipleship.

Their bonds of faith were tested but remained resilient, shaped by the enduring presence of the Holy Spirit. The imperfections of these first followers serve to encourage modern readers, demonstrating that divine purposes are fulfilled not through perfect people but through those willing to trust, follow, and be reshaped by grace.

In exploring the twelve disciples, we glimpse the fullness of the Christian journey, marked by doubt and discovery, failure and forgiveness, friendship and fidelity. Their stories invite us into a companionship with Christ that embraces human complexity and calls for total surrender. It is through their lives that the gospel advanced, through flawed yet faithful men who walked with the Son of Man and were forever changed.

Thus, the twelve disciples are more than historical figures; they are mirrors reflecting our own struggles and hopes in following Jesus. Their bonds of faith, woven amid their flaws, call us to a deeper understanding of discipleship, a journey not of perfection, but of persistent love and growth with the Savior. As we reflect on their lives, we are drawn into the heart of friendship with Christ, empowered to walk in the footsteps of those first followers who dared to leave all and embrace the eternal mission.

Parables as Living Stories

In the arid hills and dusty paths of ancient Judea, Jesus often gathered His listeners beneath the shade of olive trees or beside the calm waters of a tranquil lake. There, He spoke in stories, vivid, compelling tales that captured the imaginations of all who heard them. These parables, simple in structure yet profound in meaning, were more than mere anecdotes; they were living stories, woven with imagery and symbolism that reached beyond their immediate context to touch the eternal struggles, hopes, and truths of the human condition.

To enter into the parables is to step into a world of sensory richness and emotional depth. When Jesus tells the story of the Good Samaritan, for instance, He draws His listeners into a rugged terrain scarred by violence and neglect. Imagine the winding road from Jerusalem to Jericho, notorious for its treachery and danger, a path carved through jagged cliffs and shadowed crevices. The sun beats down relentlessly, casting long, hot rays upon the rocky ground, while the scent of dust and dry earth fills the air. Here, a man lies wounded, half-buried in the dust and blood, a victim of marauders who have left him stripped and helpless.

Into this scene first comes a priest, recognizable by the distinct garments of his office, perhaps with the softness of palm-sandaled feet upon the gravel. His face is set with concern, but to cross this forsaken road risks contamination, ritual defilement, and maybe danger. So, he passes by on the other side, his footsteps soundless but his indifference resounding. Soon after, a Levite does the same, his eyes averted, his heart distant, until it seems the man's plight is abandoned entirely.

Then arrives the Samaritan, a figure unexpected by Jesus' original hearers because of longstanding ethnic and religious tensions. He approaches not with disdain but with compassion, kneeling beside the hurt man, his hands steady and gentle as he pours oil and wine into the wounds, the healing balms of that time. His cloak becomes a bandage; his beast, a means of rescue. The Samaritan ushers the sufferer into the safety of an inn, pledging further care and covering the expenses. This is no mere tale of charity; it is a radical redefinition of neighbor, a call to love beyond boundaries, beyond prejudice.

Through words that evoke the oppressive sun, the gritty stones, the anguished moans, and the grace-filled ministrations of the Samaritan, the story leaps from Scripture into the hearts of its listeners. This is a living story, where a truth as old as compassion itself takes breath in a moment, steady and unmistakable. It is a mirror held up to the soul, reflecting back questions about who we are and who we ought to be in a fractured world.

Parallel in its evocative power and rich symbolism is the parable of the Prodigal Son, a narrative suffused with layers of emotional nuance and theological depth. Picture the household of a wealthy man in the fertile countryside, a homestead vibrant with olive groves, fig trees dropping ripe fruit, and the steady sound of laughter amid servants and kin. The younger son, restless and yearning, demands the inheritance due unto him, an act both bold and disrespectful, for dividing an estate before a father's death was both socially and morally fraught.

He departs with a heart brimming with freedom but empty of wisdom, venturing into distant lands where prosperity soon turns into desolation. There, the son squanders wealth on riotous living; the bustling markets and saloons of the city replace the serene fields of his youth. Imagine the contrast, the once proud garments now ragged, the face sunken with hunger, the echoing loneliness amid crowded streets. Famine descends, and survival demands the degrading labor of a swineherd, a job steeped in impurity for a Jew recalling his upbringing.

In the depths of despair, the son rehearses a formula of repentance, a speech that acknowledges sin and unworthiness. Yet the story turns with a sudden burst of motion: a father's gaze rests afar, scanning the horizon; at last, the figure of a wayward son appears, stumbling yet still resolute. The father runs, an extraordinary gesture breaking cultural norms of dignified restraint, and embraces the child with tears and kisses. The reverberations of forgiveness echo through the household as servants hasten to clothe the son in the best robe and prepare a feast, celebrating not only a return but a restoration.

This narrative is alive with sensory detail: the dusty road, the son's ragged clothes, the father's expansive arms, the scent of roasted meat and festive bread. Yet beneath this tangible imagery lies the spiritual truth of God's boundless mercy, the call to repentance, and the transformative power of unconditional love. It is a story that resonates still, not just through the ages but within the chambers of every heart that has wandered and longs for home.

In both parables, the artistry of Jesus' storytelling emerges powerfully. The use of everyday situations, travelers on roads, family disputes, lost possessions, feasts, and funerals grounds the moral and spiritual lessons in common experience. This accessibility is a key element of why the parables endure as living stories: they invite each hearer into the narrative, provoking reflection on familiar struggles of injustice, grace, forgiveness, and hope.

Moreover, the symbolic language carries multiple layers of meaning, which expand upon reflection. The Samaritan, once an object of scorn, becomes a model of mercy transcending ethnic and religious divisions. The father's lavish forgiveness in the Prodigal Son points toward God's extravagant grace, so unsettling in its generosity that it upends human notions of justice and worthiness. These stories are less about passive listening and more about awakening, a summons to re-examine prejudices, to embrace repentance, and to embody compassion.

The immersive quality of these parables also lies in their capacity to evoke emotional responses. The brokenness of the wounded traveler and the disgrace of the prodigal son stir empathy and discomfort. Shame and hope mingle in the narrative tension, compelling readers and hearers alike to examine their own lives. Who among us has not felt like the injured, hoping for aid? Or like the prodigal, weighed down by regret and desperate for acceptance?

Parables, therefore, function as bridges between the divine and the human. They strip away theological abstraction and replace it with the vibrant immediacy of lived experience. The Kingdom of God is not narrated as a doctrinal treatise but revealed in simple yet profound stories, inviting a participatory engagement that engages the mind, heart, and senses.

It is also worth noting the economy of the parables' narrative form. In only a brief moment, Jesus captures complex realities: societal prejudice, familial conflict, and spiritual renewal. Their succinctness makes them easy to remember and retell, contributing to their enduring presence in Christian tradition and devotion. But beneath their apparent simplicity lies an inexhaustible richness, each reading or hearing can unearth new insights, deeper layers of meaning that resonate differently depending on one's circumstances and growth in faith.

The parables' use of sensory and situational detail enhances this effect. Alongside the Good Samaritan and the Prodigal Son, other stories such as the Mustard Seed, the Sower, and the Lost Sheep employ vivid imagery, fields ripe for harvest, birds nesting among branches, branches heavy with fruit, to illustrate truths about faith, perseverance, and God's seeking love. This language appeals not only to reason but also to imagination and memory, making spiritual lessons tangible and memorable.

In recounting these parables, the narrative invites readers not only to grasp theological concepts but to enter the scene itself: to feel the burden of the wounded man, to hear the running footsteps of a forgiving father, to smell the freshness of a field ready for sowing. This sensory immersion strengthens the connection to the text, transforming the parables into living stories that echo through the corridors of time.

Consider also how the emotional nuance is crafted through the parables' dynamics of conflict and resolution. The Good Samaritan confronts indifference and danger but triumphs in mercy. The Prodigal Son's tale moves from rebellion and despair to repentance and joyous restoration. This arc reflects the human journey of brokenness and healing, sin and redemption, separation and reunion. By engaging emotionally, these narratives transcend teaching to become experiences, inviting transformation, echoing the very heart of Jesus' mission.

Beyond their initial audiences, these parables have traveled through centuries and cultures, retaining their vitality. The human themes they address, love and hate, generosity and selfishness, judgment and grace, are universal, speaking into the soul's deepest questions. This timelessness is a testament to their living nature: not bound by era or place, but constantly renewing themselves as each new listener breathes life into their truths.

Furthermore, the parables challenge the reader to see the Kingdom of God in unexpected places. The Samaritan, hated and despised by the Jewish audience, becomes the exemplar of neighborly love. The Prodigal Son's welcome home illustrates that God's grace extends beyond human merit and societal expectations. These inversions compel a reevaluation of values and relationships, making the stories agents of social and spiritual renewal.

In this way, the parables are not simply teachings to be memorized but calls to transformation, arresting interruptions in everyday life that demand response. They invite readers to align their hearts with the divine compassion exemplified by the Samaritan and the Father, to embrace the humility and courage of the prodigal's return, and to recognize the presence of God's kingdom within the ordinary and overlooked.

Indeed, to say the parables are living stories is to acknowledge their invitation to enter fully into the narrative world they create, to walk the roads, to sit at the father's table, to witness the profound acts of mercy and forgiveness. Each telling renews its power to move and instruct, engraving spiritual truths upon the soul with the vividness of a remembered moment.

As meditators upon these parables immerse themselves in the multisensory and emotive dimensions, they find themselves drawn into the rhythms of Jesus' teaching, where faith is not abstract but incarnate in stories that live and breathe with meaning. Here, the Kingdom of God is not a distant ideal but a present reality, breaking into the world through the acts and hearts of those who respond to the call of grace.

Thus, these stories stand as enduring lamps beside life's pathway, illuminating the darkness with light born of divine love. By revisiting the parables with fresh eyes and an attentive spirit, believers across epochs encounter the living Christ, who used stories not only to teach but to transform, to invite and to heal, revealing God's heart in the simplest and most profound of narratives.

In conclusion, the parables of Jesus are rightly called living stories because they transcend time and culture, bursting with sensory detail and emotional power that breathe life into ancient words. The Good Samaritan and the Prodigal Son exemplify this vitality, offering scenes rich with imagery, characters evocative of deep spiritual realities, and narratives that challenge and comfort alike. Their layers of meaning beckon each reader into a deeper reflection on grace, mercy, repentance, and love, affirming that through simple yet compelling stories, eternal truths find their home in the hearts of all who hear and believe.

Moments of Quiet Fellowship

In the quiet repose of the evening, when the day's toils had waned and the sky began its adornment with countless stars, Jesus and His followers often found themselves gathered not in the grand synagogues or bustling marketplaces, but in the simplicity of olive groves and by the flickering light of humble fires. These moments of quiet fellowship escape the grand narratives of miracles and sermons recorded with solemn gravity, yet they carry profound weight within the hearts of those who witnessed them. It is here, in these tender interludes, that the beauty of Jesus' relational ministry shines with an intimate glow, a glow born not only of divine purpose but of authentic human connection.

The days of Jesus' earthly ministry were marked by countless teachings and prodigious healings, but there was a rhythm of retreat, of sharing, and of mutual comfort woven into His journey. As the sun dipped low, casting its final amber hues upon the earth, the disciples would often find repose under the cool shade of olive trees. These trees, ancient and sturdy, spoke a silent testimony of endurance and blessing, just as the gathering beneath them was a testament to trust and friendship.

Imagine the soft rustle of olive leaves, stirred by a gentle breeze scented faintly with the fragrance of earth and ripening fruit. Around this natural canopy, Jesus sat, His countenance relaxed from the strains of public ministry, His eyes ablaze instead with kindness and attention. The disciples, weary from the day's endeavors, drew close, not in rigid solemnity, but with the ease of companions who had walked many miles together, shared meals, and bared their hearts.

In these moments, laughter was not a stranger. It echoed softly, sometimes in response to a gentle jest or a simple tale from a life long lived in Galilee's small villages. Peter, known for his impulsive spirit, might break the quiet with a boisterous tale of his near fiasco on the Sea of Galilee, prompting a chorus of smiles and a few hearty chuckles. Jesus' laughter, rich and genuine, often followed a sound recorded not in scrolls but in the recollections of those closest to Him. It was a sound of warmth and acceptance, a balm that soothed weary hearts.

But these moments were more than simply fellowship, they were a sacred space where instruction transcended formal discourse and became personal. In the soft glow of firelight, casting dancing shadows upon faces rimmed with exhaustion and hope, Jesus taught not as a distant Rabbi but as a friend who cared deeply for the growth of each soul.

Consider a night when, seated on a large stone warmed by the day, Jesus spoke quietly to John. The beloved disciple, leaning close, could feel the tenderness in the Teacher's voice as He explained the mysteries of the Kingdom of God. The language was pastoral, filled with images drawn from their common life: the small seeds sown, the vineyards tended, the shepherd who leaves the ninety and nine to seek the lost one. Each word was an invitation to trust, each parable a thread bonding their hearts.

Yet alongside trust and affection, there was correction wrapped in compassion. Jesus often used these intimate gatherings to gently unveil imperfections in His followers, not in anger or humiliation, but with a spirit of restoration. On one such evening, addressing James and John, the sons of Zebedee, He might have spoken quietly but firmly about the cost of true discipleship, about humility and service. The words, though weighty, carried no judgment; instead, they were delivered as a loving challenge, nudging His closest friends toward maturity in faith and character.

These teachings in the shadows were often accompanied by acts that spoke louder than words. Jesus broke bread with His companions, the simple loaves and small fish passing from hand to hand, each morsel shared not merely to satisfy the hunger of the body but to bind them more tightly in fellowship. The aroma of freshly baked bread mingled with the sharp tang of olive oil, and the warmth of the fire painted all of them in a gentle glow. This eating together was a sacrament of presence, an enactment of God's provision and a reminder of the community that faith builds.

The physical surroundings of these moments added layers of meaning to their time in communion. The cool night air, filled with the scent of crushed herbs and distant wildflowers, pressed gently against sun-warmed skin. Overhead, the stars burned with ancient light, endless in number and silent in their watchfulness, casting a celestial canopy that spoke silently of God's vast creation and providence. In this setting, the concerns of the world and even the pressures of ministry seemed to fall away, replaced by a shared sanctuary of peace and understanding.

These vignettes also revealed shared vulnerability, a mutual unveiling of heart that deepened their connection. Jesus, divine and yet fully human, did not stand apart behind a veil of authority; He showed His own human emotions, sorrow, compassion, and joy, in ways unmistakably real and accessible. When Martha labored anxiously over preparations for a meal, Jesus gently reminded her of the better part reserved for Mary, an attentive heart inclined toward listening and learning. This moment, observed by those near, illuminated the grace poured into everyday relationships amid ministry's demands.

Likewise, the laughter shared after a long day's journey softened any lingering tensions or doubts among the disciples. Simon's quick wit and Matthew's thoughtful observations sparked conversations that ranged from shared memories to hopes for the future. The ease of these dialogues bore witness to the profound trust Jesus had engendered in them, not because of His miraculous powers alone, but because He honored and accepted them fully, flaws and all.

In one particularly tender moment, after a day filled with heated disputes among the crowds and challenges from the Pharisees, Jesus withdrew to a quiet spot by the edge of a field. His followers sat in a semicircle, the earth beneath them cool and firm, the sky deepening to midnight blue. The silence between them was not empty but charged with a sacred weight. Breaking it softly, Jesus spoke of the Father's love not as a doctrine but as a lived reality. Tears glistened in the eyes of the disciples, moved by the simplicity and depth of His message.

Through these shared experiences, the relational fabric between Jesus and His followers was woven into something truly extraordinary. It was a tapestry threaded with joy, truth, discipline, and affection. Each moment of gentle correction was balanced by reassurance; each shared meal paved the way for deeper conversation; each smile or touch communicated a profound solidarity in mission and humanity.

Even the sensory details of these gatherings contributed to their spiritual nourishment. The warmth of the fire was not merely physical, it symbolized the Spirit's presence in their midst, igniting hope and courage. The taste of salt mixed in the bread reminded them of their call to be "the salt of the earth," preserving and flavoring the world by their faithfulness. The starry canopy above pointed their gaze heavenward, reminding them that though their feet trod dusty roads, their hearts were anchored in eternal truth.

These moments also held a powerful prophetic dimension. Though grounded in the quotidian, they prefigured the Last Supper and the new covenant Jesus would establish. The intimacy, the breaking of bread, the pouring of wine, and the mutual washing of feet found their roots in these humble scenes. The love and servant-heartedness displayed in these quiet evenings laid the foundation for the enduring fellowship that would characterize the early Church and the ongoing communion of believers throughout the ages.

The tenderness of these episodes illuminates the heart of Jesus' mission, not merely to teach or heal in isolation, but to embody the kingdom of God in tangible relationships. Each encounter was a testament to the truth that discipleship is not a solitary endeavor but a shared journey marked by laughter, tears, instruction, and grace.

In reflecting upon these moments, readers are invited to see beyond the grand narratives of miracles and teachings into the living reality of Jesus' fellowship with His friends. The power of His ministry was not only in the world-changing acts but in the daily acts of love and presence shared by fireside and olive grove. These intimate vignettes model for believers today the beauty of accompanying one another in faith, with honesty, openness, and joy.

Thus, the narrative tapestry is enriched not only by the proclamation of Kingdom truths but by the woven threads of personal companionship. It is here that the church may find one of its most enduring lessons: that the call to follow Christ involves entering into deep, tender relationships where teaching meets listening, correction meets grace, and lives are knit together by shared bread and mutual care.

The life of Jesus, therefore, pulses as much in the quiet fellowship as in the public ministry, as much in the laughter shared beneath the stars as in the solemn prayers offered alone. It is in these sacred snapshots that the divine and the human meet fully, revealing the heart of the Savior who calls His followers not just to believe, but to belong, to lives intertwined with His and one another's through moments of joy, learning, correction, and love.

The Journey to Jerusalem: Shadows Ascend

Approaching the Holy City

As the weary band of travelers pressed onward, the path toward Jerusalem lay heavy with portent. The sun, once bright and welcoming in the east, now weakened beneath thickening veils of shifting gray, as if the heavens themselves prepared a somber curtain for the unfolding drama. Fading daylight seeped languidly through layers of oppressive clouds, casting the earth in an elusive twilight that neither embraced day nor welcomed night. This was no ordinary journey; it was a solemn pilgrimage, burdened with the weight not only of mundane travel but also of an approaching destiny that neither the disciples nor the crowds fully comprehended.

The countryside, once alive with spring's vibrant blooms and the laughter of distant shepherds, had taken on an austere aspect. Fields of ripened grain bent silently in muted breezes, their golden stalks dulled beneath the heavy sky. Olive trees, ancient and twisted, stood like sentinels along the slopes, their gnarled limbs reaching toward a horizon shadowed and uncertain. Even the birds seemed to pause in their flight, their songs tapering to quiet murmurs as the company of Jesus and His followers pressed toward the city that had long been the center of their nation's hopes and sorrows.

Among the company, a palpable tension simmered beneath the surface. The disciples walked with eyes fixed both forward and downward, their faces etched with lines of perplexity and unease. Some exchanged furtive glances, while others regarded the Teacher with a mix of reverence and apprehension. Each step closer to Jerusalem seemed to draw a heavier cloak around their hearts, a weight woven from the threads of prophecy, expectation, and the gathering storm of opposition.

Jesus, too, was not untouched by the gravity of the moment. Though His face remained calm and resolute, there lay in His eyes depths of sorrow and determination. The same lips that had commanded storms and healed the sick were now pressed in quiet resolve, fully aware of the path ahead, the path steeped with suffering, sacrifice, and ultimately, resurrection. His journey was not merely a physical approach to a city of stone and temple; it was an entrance into the defining act of God's redemptive plan.

As they neared the outskirts of Jerusalem, the din and clamor of the city began to ebb into their consciousness. From a distance, the white limestone walls gleamed faintly beneath the dulling sky, the citadel perched like a crown upon the mount. Yet beneath this gleaming veneer, shadows lurked. Political tensions brimmed among the rulers, and religious authorities whispered in hushed chambers, their plans tightening like a snare. Rumors raced swiftly through the streets as the populace debated with fervor: "Who is this Jesus who comes with such authority? What claim does He hold that draws multitudes wherever He treads?" Fear and hope intermingled in equal measure, but all sensed the whirlwind fast approaching.

Prophetic warnings, etched in the words of the old prophets, echoed in the memories of the disciples. "Behold, your King cometh unto you, meek, and sitting upon an ass," they recalled, even as reports came of rising hostility among the Pharisees and Sadducees. The scales of justice and mercy seemed poised to tip, as the spiritual and political forces of the city braced themselves for what some deemed an inevitable confrontation. The long-awaited Messiah was arriving, yet the acceptance He sought was shrouded in a veil of misunderstanding and resistance.

Each step deeper into Judean soil seemed to pull the shadows longer, as if the very earth conspired to cloak this coming moment in mystery and trial. The dusty road was lined by olive trees whose branches cast flickering shapes against the darkening horizon, shapes that seemed to foreshadow the struggle between light and darkness poised on the precipice. The fading sun, obscured by gathering clouds, mirrored the dimming hope of those who yearned for deliverance but feared its cost.

The murmurs from the city streets grew louder, carried on waves of suspicion and expectation. Merchants shuttered their stalls earlier than usual, wary eyes watching the route Jesus and His followers might take. The Temple, the heart of Jewish worship and identity, was a place of tension, a rubbing stone where religious fervor and political control ground hard against each other. The Sanhedrin moved covertly, their deliberations increasing in urgency and resolve. Within this sacred yet turbulent city, the teacher from Galilee would soon be tested not just by their words but by the full force of the empire's power.

Among the crowds following Jesus, there was a growing dichotomy of fervor and fear. Some hailed Him as the promised King, waving palm branches and singing praises in anticipation of liberation from Roman rule. Others questioned quietly, whispering warnings to hold back expectations lest they kindle the fire of unrest and bring swift retaliation. The air was thick with a restless energy, hope intertwined with dread, faith shadowed by misunderstanding.

In the faces of the disciples, collective anxieties found expression in confused debate and hesitant questions. Peter, whose boldness often led the way, furrowed his brow at the omens and teachings Jesus had repeatedly spoken of suffering, rejection, and resurrection. Thomas, ever cautious, wrestled silently with doubts, seeking assurance that the path into the city was not one paved with destruction but with salvation. Judas, cloaked in an inscrutable silence, carried secrets and motives veiled beneath the surface, foreshadowing the tragic betrayal to come.

Throughout this somber convoy, Jesus walked with a measured pace that belied the storm within, a storm that had begun in the Garden of Gethsemane and would soon reach its tragic climax upon the hill called Golgotha. His words, few but deliberate, gave glimpses into the future: prophecies of the crucifixion, warnings to the cities that rejected Him, and assurances of the kingdom that transcended earthly power. These utterances puzzled many then, but they rang clear to those whose eyes began to see beyond the temporal.

The imagery of gathering shadows was not lost upon those who listened intently to the Master's teaching. As the sun sank lower behind the rugged hills, the very air seemed charged with a sacred gravity, the darkening horizon a visual psalm of the spiritual contest enveloping the land. Darkness was rising, yet within that darkness glimmered the promise of dawn. For the shadow of the cross hovered near, but so too did the light of resurrection.

Even the natural world bore silent witness to this journey toward destiny. The wind whispered through the leaves with a spectral breath, as though carrying the sighs of prophets long silent. The earth beneath, once vibrant, seemed to hush in anticipation, holding its breath as the hour of divine appointment drew nigh. The heavens, smothered beneath cloud and shadow, foreshadowed the turmoil of the coming days, where sky and earth alike would cry out in grief and awe.

As the company of Jesus drew closer to Jerusalem's gates, the air became thick with a sense of closing chapters and opening mysteries. The city, ancient and sacred, stood at the crossroads of history and eternity. Here, kings and priests, thieves and martyrs, had made their mark upon the stones; now the greatest story was to unfold where all threads of prophecy converged. The pilgrim steps of the Messiah stirred the dust, but more profoundly stirred the age-old conflict between flesh and spirit, law and grace, death and life.

The scene was set with all the tension of a theater poised at the threshold of its defining act. The crowds, swelling on the road and growing restless in the hills, were a living chorus of expectation and fear. The leaders, cloaked in robes of authority, sharpened their tongues and tightened their schemes. And Jesus, resolute and calm, moved steadily forward, toward the city that would test Him, condemn Him, and ultimately witness the triumph of God's eternal love.

In this confluence of human history and divine purpose, approaching Jerusalem was more than arrival at a place; it was entering a spiritual battlefield where the forces of darkness sought to extinguish the Light, yet would unwittingly herald its unstoppable dawn. As the pilgrim band crossed from the wilderness into the shadowed sanctuary of the city, the fading light and leaden sky bore silent witness to the sacred passage from promise to fulfillment, from prophecy to resurrection.

Thus, the journey unfolded: a solemn pilgrimage, a heavy tread toward the shadowed city, where the Savior's destiny would be shaped by rejection and love, death and victory. The road was lined with shadows, but steadfast hope burned within every step, promising that even the darkest hour was but the threshold of dawn. And so, with hearts burdened yet bold, the company of Jesus approached Jerusalem, the holy city awaiting the passage from an age of sorrow into the radiant dawn of redemption.

Triumphal Entry: Hosannas and Hushed Reversals

The sun hung low along the dusty horizon, casting long, golden rays that filtered through the rustling palm fronds. A gentle breeze stirred the air, carrying the scent of freshly trampled earth and the faint aroma of wildflowers from the surrounding hills. The road to Jerusalem, a ribbon of well-worn stone and compacted dirt, stretched ahead, a path both familiar and fraught with expectation. Along this ancient route, a gathering thronged, eager and animated, as word spread that Jesus of Nazareth was drawing near.

Palm branches in trembling hands swayed with the rhythm of an unfolding moment. Their leaves whispered softly, a susurration of verdant celebration that flourished under the brightening sky. A chorus of voices rose, vibrant and unrestrained, a tempest of shouts and cries that seemed scarcely contained by human lungs alone. "Hosanna! Hosanna to the Son of David! Blessed is he that cometh in the name of the Lord! Hosanna in the highest!" Their exultation filled the air with a sacred fervor, a jubilant tide lifting spirits and hopes alike.

Amidst the throng, the figure of Jesus appeared, ascending steadily toward the city that pulsed with anticipation and ancient power. Mounted upon a colt, unadorned and humble, He bore the gravity of destiny without haste or ostentation. His eyes, calm and steady, scanned the sea of faces, some radiant with joy and faith, others shadowed by doubt and quiet apprehension. The measured dignity with which He rode bespoke a royal majesty not recognized by all, yet unmistakably present to those who looked beyond the surface.

The colt's hooves stirred up a swirl of dust, sunlight catching grains aloft like fleeting sparks. The sound of approaching feet, the shuffle of sandals on stone, the clamor of voices, the crackle of palm fronds breaking in eager hands, formed a symphony of life and fervor. Children ran ahead, their laughter mingling with shouts; elders raised their hands in blessing; young men sang songs of prophecy and hope passed down through the ages.

The jubilations were not merely expressions of adulation; they were a collective breath held on the cusp of fulfillment. To many, this moment signified the long-awaited dawn of a kingdom that would restore Israel, a balm to sufferings endured under Roman rule and the corruption of religious elites. The titles proclaimed, "Son of David,"

"King of Israel," "Messiah", evoked the legacy of kings and prophets, a heritage laden with promises ancient and divine.

Yet beneath this radiant canopy of praise stirred quieter currents, shrouded in shadow and uncertainty. Among the crowd moved watchers too wary to join in ecstatic cries, scribes and Pharisees, temple guards and Roman sympathizers. Their eyes narrowed, fingers tapped and folded into scrutinizing postures, hearts wrestling fear with suspicion. For they perceived, though they dared not proclaim, that this humble procession bore a challenge as much as a celebration. A challenge not just to earthly authorities but to divine order itself.

The sanctity of the moment was paradoxical, a tapestry woven of adulation and unease, expectation and trepidation. Every chorus of "Hosanna" echoed against an undercurrent of whispered counsel in dim corners, plotting that which might soon bring a crushing silence. The city walls, venerable and storied, seemed to hold their breath along with the gathering throng.

Jesus's entrance into Jerusalem was more than a mere arrival; it was an irruption of sacred history into present reality, a living prophecy unfolding in flesh and blood. As He moved forward, the hopes and fears of a nation entwined around Him, each heart a note in a song of anticipation and profound contradiction.

The sensory mosaic of the scene abounded with vivid detail. The sharp fragrance of crushed palm leaves mingled with the distant murmur of temple worship, the occasional peal of a bell from a passing caravan, and the murmur of water from nearby springs. Sounds and scents wove an immersive backdrop to the unfolding drama, anchoring the spiritual in tangible reality.

The voices of the crowd rose and fell like a living wave. Some cried out with joyous abandon, their voices cracking with emotion; others intoned from memory, reciting Psalms and scriptures that foretold of a coming King who would save and judge. "Blessed be the kingdom of our father David, that cometh in the name of the Lord; peace in heaven, and glory in the highest," they chanted, their Hebrew words ringing clear, ancient yet alive.

Amid the throng, individuals bore varied expressions. A woman with tear-streaked cheeks clutched a child close, whispering prayers learned from her parents; a soldier tightened his grip on his spear, his eyes flickering between awe and duty; a merchant watched carefully from a nearby stall, weighing the season's fortunes against the swelling tides of unrest.

As Jesus proceeded, the colt beneath Him moved with sure-footed grace, its unassuming nature underscoring the striking humility of the moment. Unlike the triumphal entries of earthly kings, there were no pompous chariots or banners adorned with gold. Instead, the King of kings rode upon a beast of burden, fulfilling the prophecy of Zechariah: "Behold, thy King cometh unto thee: he is just, and having salvation; lowly, and riding upon an ass."

This profound humility was both a revelation and a mystery. To the joyous crowd, it was a sign of gentle deliverance, a hope for peace; to the wary few, an unsettling enigma that defied their expectations of power. What manner of kingdom would this be if not one of sword and conquest, but of quiet strength and sacrificial love?

As the pathway ascended toward the city gates, the momentum of the crowd swelled. The pavement, worn smooth by generations, seemed to pulse beneath the feet and hooves, a prepared stage for an event both joyous and tragic. The city walls echoed back the sound of the approaching multitude, reverberating as if the stones themselves recognized the import.

The accompaniment of palm branches extended beyond mere decoration, it was a symbolic act, proclaiming allegiance to a sovereign and celebrating deliverance. Palm branches had long been emblems of victory and festivity among the Jewish people, harkening back to the feast of Tabernacles and earlier messianic hopes. To wave them was to shout with arms of leafy splendor, "This is the one foretold, the hoped-for Christ!"

The cries of "Hosanna," meaning "Save now," carried a layered meaning, an urgent plea for salvation intertwined with praise. The crowd beseeched their Messiah to bring deliverance, both political and spiritual, to liberate Israel from its manifold oppressions. Yet, even as they raised their voices, the full scope of salvation they sought remained veiled.

The contrast between the exuberant welcome and the restrained composure of Jesus created a human tension palpable in the air. His gaze was steady, imbued with the weight of knowledge that the hour of trial approached. Beneath the warmth of applause lay the cold shadow of imminent rejection. In His heart, the jubilant shouts were joined by the silent recognition of the path ahead, a path that would lead through passion, sacrifice, and resurrection.

In the midst of celebration, the undercurrents of divine purpose moved invisibly, orchestrating this moment with timeless design. Humanity's cries for a king intertwined with the eternal will of God, creating a complex weave where joy, sorrow, hope, and judgment converged. The jubilant hosannas were the sound of a people caught between the promise and peril of redemption.

As He neared the temple mount, Jesus's entrance took on a palpable gravity. The place was sacred ground, a focal point of national faith and identity. The crowd's energy, though still exultant, tightened with an edge of solemnity. Here, the hope of a nation would collide with the realities of power and prophecy, setting the stage for confrontation.

The disciples, who had followed closely, shared in the mix of exaltation and unease. Their voices joined the chorus, tempered by reverence and a dawning understanding of the magnitude of what lay ahead. They glanced at one another, sensing that the jubilant cries might soon give way to silence, and that the man they hailed as King was about to fulfill a destiny beyond their comprehension.

Beyond the city gates, observers of varied stations kept watch. The chief priests and scribes exchanged worried glances, aware that this moment threatened to unravel their fragile control. The Roman procurator, informed by reports, prepared to consider the implications for imperial order. Throughout the crowd and the wider city, the tension between celebration and suspicion simmered.

The atmosphere that day was therefore not a simple scene of victory, but a sacred juxtaposition: triumphs intertwined with reversals, hosannas alive alongside hushed deliberations. The crowd's praise ignited the hope of deliverance; the shadowed glances foretold the coming hour of decision.

In the midst of this stirring scene, the image of Jesus on the colt remains eternal: a portrait of serene dignity and kingdom purpose, meeting on that ordinary street the extraordinary expectations of a waiting world. His journey to Jerusalem, into the heart of the city, into the living temple of both stone and spirit, was marked by a complex dance of celebration and confrontation, of human hope and divine will.

The rustling palms, the thunderous shouts, and the measured steps of the humble King all converge in this timeless snapshot. They invite the reader not only to witness but to enter the emotional and spiritual crescendo of a multifaceted moment, the arrival of the Messiah amid hosannas, under whispered schemes, on the cusp of history's greatest reversal.

Teachings and Controversies in the Temple

The sun stood high over Jerusalem, casting long shadows across the ancient stones of the temple courts. The sacred precincts buzzed with activity, merchants hawking their wares, pilgrims offering sacrifices, scribes debating interpretations, all beneath the sweeping colonnades, the towering pillars, and the gleaming courts where generations had come to pray, worship, and seek communion with God. The air was thick with incense, voices rising in prayer, and the murmurs of barter and dispute. Into this vibrant but volatile setting stepped Jesus of Nazareth, His countenance calm yet resolute, eyes shining with righteous purpose as He walked through the courts of the Lord's house.

From the moment Jesus entered the temple precincts during this final journey to Jerusalem, a change swept through the atmosphere. It was as though the very stones sensed the fullness of time and the weight of destiny pressing upon the city. Eyes, sharp with suspicion and hostility, watched Him from shadowed corners. To those accustomed to the temple's rhythms, Jesus's presence was a challenge; to Him, it was the fulfillment of purpose, a platform for truth, a stage for confrontation, and a foretaste of the sacrifice soon to come.

The temple, majestic and steeped in sacred history, was more than a building. Crafted with exquisite artistry, its white marble reflected the blazing sun, columns of jasper and onyx framed the inner courts, and golden cherubim adorned the walls where once the Ark of the Covenant had rested. Yet beneath this outward splendor, corruption festered. Within the courts crowded the moneychangers and sellers of doves, their tables laden with coins and offerings, exchanging Roman currency for shekels acceptable in the treasury. Their voices, loud and persistent, pierced the sanctity, turning worship into commerce.

Jesus's steps quickened as He entered the Court of the Gentiles, the outermost area where all could approach the temple, regardless of nation. Here the noise swelled, and the traffic was thick. Merchants shouted their prices, buyers haggled intensely; tokens clinked, and the clamor of human greed and ambition mingled with the prayers and laments of the faithful pilgrims. With a voice suddenly clear and commanding, both a rebuke and a proclamation, Jesus began to overturn the tables of the moneychangers, scattering coins across the stone pavement. To those nearby, His action seemed almost violent, a disruption of the established order.

"Make not My Father's house a house of merchandise," He declared, His voice piercing over the din, echoing the ancient warnings of the prophets. His words cut deeper than any sword. They revealed a corruption beneath the surface piety, a sacrilegious mingling of devotion and profiteering that sullied the temple's sanctity. The moneychangers, caught off guard, retreated, murmuring among themselves in indignation. The sellers of doves also withdrew, their cages rattling as they were abandoned; freedom bought through fright.

Crowds gathered swiftly, drawn equally by curiosity and commotion. Whispers ran through the air: Who was this man who dared disrupt the sacred marketplace? His boldness challenged the religious authorities, the chief priests, scribes, and elders, who observed from a distance, their faces dark with anger and apprehension. The temple grounds had long been their domain, a place where tradition and power intertwined. Jesus's intrusion was an affront to their authority and an invitation to confrontation.

In the days that followed, within the very heart of the temple courts, Jesus engaged repeatedly with these religious leaders. Their questions were cunning, meant to trap Him; His answers were piercing, revealing their hypocrisy and ignorance. They asked Him by what authority He did these things. Jesus replied with a question: "The baptism of John, was it from heaven, or of men?" Caught between public opinion and their fear of losing standing, they could offer no answer, and Jesus's silence held them condemned. His words were not merely defensive; they exposed the spiritual blindness that kept them opposed to the truth.

The temple precincts became a theater of escalating tension. To the crowd, Jesus's teaching was a breath of fresh air, a revelation of the love and justice of God untainted by ritualistic emptiness. He spoke often in parables, using images drawn from the very land and life around them to unveil truths hidden from those who refused to see. One such parable told of a vineyard owner and his wicked tenants, a story that pierced the self-righteousness of the leaders and predicted their own judgment.

"This is the heir," Jesus said in the parable, "come, let us kill him, that the inheritance may be ours." The weight of His message dragged heavy upon the air: those entrusted with God's people had become like thieves, seeking to seize what was not theirs, rejecting and even plotting against God's own Son. His words summoned judgment, but also justice and hope, weaving a tapestry of divine sovereignty and human responsibility.

Amid these exchanges, Jesus also gave solemn warnings about hypocrisy and the outward show of righteousness unaccompanied by the truth of the heart. In vibrant and scathing words, collected in what would be remembered as the woes against the scribes and Pharisees, He exposed their love for honor and esteem, their long prayers made to be seen, and their neglect of mercy and faithfulness. "Ye serpents, ye generation of vipers, how can ye escape the damnation of hell?" His voice rang with sorrow and anger; behind the condemnation was a plea for repentance and a call back to genuine faith.

The temple's holy courts, in which God's presence was revered, now echoed with voices of accusation and defense, confrontation and revelation. Jesus's teaching itself became a crucible for the people's hearts: to follow Him meant crossing thresholds of understanding and faith that few were prepared to enter. His knowledge of the law went deeper than the letter, piercing to the spirit; His authority was unmistakable because it came from the Father.

As the festival of the Passover drew nearer, the weight of the confrontations grew heavier, the air charged with anticipation and danger. Jesus's actions in the temple and His searing words had stirred a tempest within the city's religious establishment. The chief priests and elders met in secret, plotting how to arrest and destroy Him. The temple, which had once been a place of peace and worship, was now shadowed by the approach of betrayal and sacrifice.

Yet even in the midst of conflict, Jesus's presence was a beacon of light. His teachings spoke not only of judgment but of the Kingdom of God, a realm where love, mercy, and righteousness reigned supreme. He challenged not only the authorities but the common people to look beyond the outer forms, to seek the will of God with sincerity and a humble heart.

Throughout the temple courts, among the sacred stones echoing the footsteps of the faithful, the battle between truth and falsehood, light and darkness, became palpable. This sacred ground was the stage upon which the eternal drama of salvation unfolded. The confrontations and teachings here were not merely historical events but the fulfillment of God's plan, a revelation of His justice and grace in the flesh.

The temple itself, once the undisputed center of Jewish worship, was confronted by the living Word made flesh. And though the authorities sought to silence Him, His voice would not be stilled. The teachings and controversies in the temple foreshadowed the greater conflict to come, the passion, the crucifixion, and the resurrection. They were the final lines of a divine dialogue written in stone and in human hearts, pointing all who heard to the ultimate truth: that God's kingdom was at hand, and that judgment and salvation walked hand in hand upon those hallowed courts.

The Last Supper's Sacred Feast

Preparation and Gathering

In the quiet shadow of twilight, the city of Jerusalem began to settle into a stillness that belied the night's solemn significance. The narrow streets, worn smooth by countless feet, echoed softly as a few last merchants closed their stalls, and the aromatic smoke from fires mingled with the brisk air descending from the hills. At the heart of this ancient city, behind a modest door tucked away on an upper floor of a stone house, the stage was set for an event that would forever mark the course of history. The upper room, a sanctified space prepared with painstaking care, awaited the arrival of Jesus and His disciples. Here, the familiar rhythms of hospitality intertwined seamlessly with an overwhelming sense of impending sorrow and profound mystery.

Within this room, the flickering candlelight cast dancing shadows upon the rough plastered walls, the feeble flames struggling against the encroaching darkness. The soft glow illuminated the worn wood of a low table around which a dozen or so men would soon gather. The air was thick with the mingled scents of fresh herbs, mint, parsley, and hyssop, laid carefully in small bowls, reminders of the Passover traditions yet also symbols laden with deeper meaning. The rising fragrance of freshly baked bread, still warm from the oven, promised nourishment but also foreshadowed the body that Jesus would offer. The simple meal prepared was more than sustenance; it was a tangible expression of covenant and sacrifice, tethered to centuries of sacred memory.

Soft murmurs drifted through the room, the hushed voices of those preparing the feast blending reverently with the faint sounds of the city outside. The disciples had scattered throughout the day to secure the necessary provisions, but as the evening deepened, most returned, some bearing trays of unleavened bread, others with cups filled with new wine. Their movements were deliberate, subdued, as if each act held a weight far beyond ordinary preparation. The usual clamor and laughter that might mark such a gathering were replaced by a solemn, contemplative stillness, the tension beneath the surface unmistakable.

Among those aiding in the preparations was Mary Magdalene, whose presence brought a quiet warmth to the chamber. Though the biblical narratives do not specify her role in this precise moment, it is reasonable to envision her attentive hands arranging the herbs or quietly setting the vessels, her heart heavy with both devotion and a creeping unease. Mary's story, marked by deliverance and unwavering faith, reflected the human warmth and sacred anticipation that infused the room. Her gaze lingered on the door, waiting, knowing that the coming hours would forever alter the lives of all present.

Other women, some unnamed, moved with reverent urgency, their tasks humble yet crucial. Bowls were filled and pastries placed on plates; cups were washed and polished until they gleamed under the candlelight. These acts, carried out with quiet dedication, underscored a profound humanity that bridged the divine and the earthly. The flickering light caught glimpses of faces marked by mixed emotions, hope, fear, love, and a dawning realization of the gravity ahead.

The walls of that upper room bore silent witness to more than the gathering for the Passover meal. They enclosed a sacred threshold between the familiar and the unknown, between tradition and fulfillment, between the joys of fellowship and the anguish of sacrifice. Each item in the room, from the linen cloth draped over the table to the earthenware jars standing in corners, became a signpost on a spiritual journey reaching back to the exodus of Israel and forward into the new covenant Jesus was to establish.

As the hour approached, footsteps echoed on the stairs, and a door opened softly. One by one, the disciples entered, their features illuminated by the soft glow of the candles. Their expressions were taut and somber, betraying the undercurrent of anxiety and sorrow they sought to mask. Among them, Peter's confident gaze wrestled with unease, and John's quiet presence seemed tinged with a melancholy that words could not convey. Judas Iscariot entered with a measured pace, his countenance guarded and inscrutable, adding a layer of complexity to the atmosphere.

The air grew heavier with expectation, an unspoken acknowledgment that this was no ordinary meal but a profound act of remembrance and revelation. The faithful recounting of the Exodus was at its heart a memorial to God's mighty hand in delivering His people, yet on this night, it would also become the poignant setting for Jesus to reveal the true nature of that deliverance, one that transcended history and entered eternity.

The disciples seated themselves around the table, the circle incomplete without the Master's arrival. Their whispers faded into silence as a figure appeared in the doorway, a presence that commanded both reverence and love. Jesus entered, His countenance serene yet shadowed by the knowledge of what was to come. The room seemed to hold its breath. The sacred feast was about to begin.

There was a palpable tension mingled with tenderness, a moment suspended between the sacred tradition of Passover and the revolutionary act that Jesus was about to perform. As He moved to wash the feet of His disciples, a gesture of humble service and love, the atmosphere shifted imperceptibly, infusing the room with a deeper sense of purpose. The external preparations gave way to an internal gathering of souls, a preparation not only of space and sustenance but of hearts and minds.

The upper room, with its flickering candlelight, fragrant herbs, and the restful murmur of those who prepared it, was transformed into a sanctuary of divine revelation. Here, the boundary between the temporal and the eternal blurred, and the sacred feast became a foretaste of the kingdom to come. The tension of the night unfolded not as mere human tragedy but as the passage through which redemption would be wrought.

Throughout those hours of preparation and gathering, the mingled scents, the gentle movements, and the quiet conversations bore witness to the weighty significance of what was to transpire. It was more than a meal postponed or a ritual fulfilled; it was the manifestation of God's steadfast love, the inauguration of a new covenant sealed not in stone but in flesh and blood.

In capturing these moments, the narrative draws not only from the Gospel accounts but seeks to give voice and depth to the silent spaces between the recorded words, the human warmth of those who loved Jesus, their fearful hope, and the sacred anticipation that filled that upper room. It invites the reader into the intimacy of a scene both ordinary in its setting and extraordinary in its purpose, setting the contemplative and sacred tone for the Last Supper's unfolding mystery.

Words of Covenant and Communion

The flickering glow of oil lamps cast a trembling light upon the faces gathered within the upper room. Shadows danced upon the rough-hewn walls, as if to echo the silent tremors of the human heart, awe mingled with sorrow, devotion entwined with the weight of what was unfolding. In this room, on the night sacred beyond all others, Jesus of Nazareth sat with His disciples, marking the moment that would forever change the course of human history. The scene is at once tender and transcendent, a tableau of covenant and communion that reaches beyond the confines of time.

Jesus had, just moments prior, washed the feet of those He was about to leave, an act of humility no master had stooped to perform for men who had been His companions, His friends, His chosen apostles. Yet now a more profound rite awaited: the breaking of bread, the sharing of wine, and the pronouncing of words that would illuminate the meaning of sacrifice and redemption in a way that would echo through all generations.

The bread, simple, unleavened, baked for the feast of Passover, was lifted by the Master's hands. He broke it deliberately, with a solemnity that caught the room's very breath. "Take, eat: this is my body," Jesus said, His voice steady, suffused with grave tenderness. The disciples looked on, some bewildered, others intent, as if trying to grasp the profound mystery concealed in these words. What did it mean that this loaf, common among meals, was now His body? That this sharing would transcend physical nourishment, becoming a spiritual lifeline?

The body, He intimated, was not merely flesh and bone. It was the embodiment of the new covenant, a living sacrifice offered not by priests in the temple, but by Himself, the Son of Man. The body that would soon hang upon a cross, bruised and broken, was now made present in this moment, broken for those He loved. The breaking of bread was itself a sacrament of the coming passion, a symbol of the pain that would soon be poured out and the life that would be given. To partake of this bread was to remember, not only a ritual command to recall a past event, but an invitation to enter into the reality of Jesus's sacrifice, to join in the divine plan of redemption that reached beyond time into eternity.

Then, passing the cup, Jesus spoke again: "Drink ye all of it; for this is my blood of the new testament, which is shed for many for the remission of sins." The wine shimmered darkly in the cup, a tangible symbol of the blood soon to be spilled, the blood of the covenant, blood that sealed the promise between God and man. His words carried a dual weight: the immediacy of impending suffering and the eternal scope of mercy and grace poured forth in the shedding of His blood.

In ancient Israel, the shedding of blood was the foundation of every covenant. It was through sacrifice that relationships were bound, through the offering of bulls and goats and lambs that the people's sins were covered, temporary peace restored. Now, Jesus declared, a new covenant was being inaugurated, not with the blood of animals, but with His own. This covenant was perfect, definitive, and eternal. It was a covenant of love and forgiveness, extending the mercy of God to all who would receive it. The cup was not merely wine; it was death and life mingled into one, a pledge of spiritual sustenance for the soul.

As He shared the cup, the disciples' eyes met His. Within that small circle, time seemed suspended. The raw mixture of emotions, sorrow for the suffering ahead, awe at the depth of divine love, hope in the promise of resurrection, painted every face. Even Judas sat there, the betrayer, caught in a moment heavy with quiet anguish and unspoken betrayal. Jesus's gaze, steady and searching, seemed to pierce the human heart, knowing each secret struggle and frailty.

The scene transcended the mere telling of a story; it became an invitation. An invitation to all present, and to all readers through the centuries, to step beyond passive observers and enter into this covenant of grace. To partake of the bread and wine is not only to remember but to be made partakers in the life, death, and resurrection of Christ. In this sacred feast, Jesus invited His followers to a fellowship that bridged heaven and earth, heaven's holiness poured into earthly vessels.

There was a profound intimacy in Jesus's words, even as they bore the weight of cosmic significance. The phrasing, "This do in remembrance of me," was at once simple and majestic. It was a command, yes, but also a tender plea. To remember was to live anew, to keep alive the story of love that saves and redeems. It was to hold close the mystery of a God who humbled Himself to bear the sins of the world, a God who chose suffering over sovereignty, the cross over the crown.

Throughout the millennia, believers have returned again and again to this moment. The breaking of bread and sharing of the cup have become more than ritual acts; they are the living heartbeat of Christian worship. Each Eucharist, each communion service, is a re-presentation of the original covenant, a renewing of the bond between Christ and His Church. The bread and wine are both physical sustenance and earthly signs of a spiritual truth, that through Christ's body given and His blood shed, believers are united in His life and love.

The passage from the King James Bible preserves a majesty and solemnity in Jesus's words that powerfully convey this significance:

"And he took bread, and gave thanks, and brake it, and gave unto them, saying, This is my body which is given for you: this do in remembrance of me. Likewise also the cup after supper, saying, This cup is the new testament in my blood, which is shed for you." (Luke 22:19-20)

Within these lines lies the heart of the gospel itself, tender, sacrificial, covenantal. The Greek word translated as "new testament" (διαθήκη, diathēkē) means covenant; it conveys not merely a document or promise, but a living relationship sealed by blood. This new covenant would surpass and fulfill the old, offering access to God not through temple rites, but through the very person of Jesus, His life poured out as a once-and-for-all atonement for sin.

The breaking of bread and sharing of the cup were therefore not only acts of remembrance but acts of participation. Jesus's disciples, then and now, partake of His body and blood in faith, drawing near to His sacrifice and sharing in the fruits of redemption. Through this holy meal, the believer is enveloped in grace, bound to Christ, and united with the Church universal.

The atmosphere of the upper room, charged with this divine revelation, reveals much about the nature of the covenant itself. It is both solemn and joyful, sorrowful and hopeful. Jesus's words echo through the chambers of eternity: the body broken and blood shed were foretold in prophecy, made manifest in history, and now lived out in the hearts of those who believe. The covenant is unbreakable because it rests not on human fidelity, but on divine faithfulness.

Moreover, the Eucharistic feast reflects the profound unity of God's plan. It is not an isolated moment but the consummation of salvation history, from the Passover lamb sacrificed in Egypt to the ultimate Lamb of God who takes away the sin of the world. Christ's institution of this sacred meal reinterpreted ancient symbols, transforming bread and wine into emblems of new life, new hope, and new covenant intimacy.

The tactile elements, the loaf, the cup, ground the sacred in the familiar. They remind the disciples, and all believers, that God's grace is not abstract or distant but comes to us in tangible form. As one breaks the bread and drinks the wine, so too is one nourished spiritually. The body becomes the source of spiritual strength, and the blood the seal of forgiveness and renewal.

In the silence that follows these words, the disciples and readers alike encounter a divine paradox: the path to eternal life lies through death; the greatest strength is shown in surrender; the deepest union is forged in sacrifice. To accept the bread and wine is to enter into this paradox and find in it hope, healing, and transformation.

The covenant Jesus proclaims is enduring. It is a promise to those who gather around the table, to those whose faith is small or great, to all who come with contrite hearts. Time and again, Christians have returned to this feast in times of joy and despair, in moments of clarity and doubt, finding in the "Words of Covenant and Communion" a source of steadfast love and divine presence.

Beyond the theological depth, this moment reveals the heart of Jesus himself. In the quiet breaking of bread and passing of the cup, He expresses a love that is entirely self-giving. It is the love that "layeth down his life for his friends" (John 15:13), the love that commands no greater honor than to lay down one's life. His words are spoken not from a distant throne but from the same table where friendship and fellowship are lived out. This intimacy calls forth the entire assembly, then, now, and forever, to live as a community shaped by sacrifice, marked by grace, and sustained by remembrance.

Thus, the "Words of Covenant and Communion" are much more than historical utterances. They constitute the living heart of Christian worship, the source and summit of discipleship, and the ever-unfolding encounter with Christ's redeeming love. When the bread is broken and the cup is shared, believers enter that sacred upper room, surrounded by faces etched with awe, sorrow, and devotion, feeling the covenant's weight settle over their souls. In that sacred moment, the divine mystery becomes accessible, God with us, in us, through us, transforming bread and wine into the eternal pledge of life everlasting.

To participate in this meal is therefore to be invited into a sacred story that claims us and changes us. It is the covenant written, the promise fulfilled, the communion shared, a feast not only of sustenance but of salvation, not only of remembrance but of living truth. This is the sacred feast of the Last Supper, where history, heaven, and heart converge around words that speak eternally: "This is my body... This is my blood... Do this in remembrance of me."

Betrayal Foretold and a Night of Vigil

As the Last Supper drew to its solemn close, a stillness settled upon the chamber. The flickering light of lamps cast trembling shadows across the faces gathered around the table, where moments earlier, Jesus had shared bread and wine, symbols of a new covenant. Yet, beneath the veneer of fellowship, a tension thickened the air, an unspoken dread palpable in every measured breath. It was in this charged silence that Jesus spoke, unveiling the dark portent that would soon shadow their lives, a betrayal from within their own midst.

His voice, steady yet weighed with sorrow, broke the quiet. "Verily, verily, I say unto you, that one of you shall betray me." The words hung heavy, a whispered thunder over the room. The disciples, who moments before had been united in reverence and love, now found their gaze flitting uneasily, searching one another's eyes for truth and loyalty. The statement was not a mere prediction but a piercing arrow aimed at the heart of their fellowship. Each man wrestled privately with suspicion, confusion, and an aching disbelief that such treachery could come from a brother.

Peter, ever passionate and impulsive, leaned forward, his voice edged with both fervor and desperation: "Lord, is it I?" The rest echoed his question in murmurs of doubt and denial, their bodies tensing as the gravity of the accusation sank deep. Yet Jesus's words offered neither clarity nor comfort, only the somber confirmation that the traitor walked among them, cloaked in the familiar guise of friendship.

In this moment, the psychology of betrayal unfolded with acute subtlety. Suspicion bred a quiet turmoil in the disciples' hearts. Eyes darted furtively; gestures became spasmodic, as if the very act of watching one another might unmask a hidden foe. The intimacy of their shared meal was shattered by an invisible fracture running through their circle, isolating each man within his own restless thoughts. The scene was not of outward violence but of an internal tempest, a spiritual and emotional crisis that revealed the deepest vulnerabilities of their fellowship.

Yet amid this fragile atmosphere, Jesus remained calm, a pillar of unyielding resolve. His gaze moved past the anxious faces, fixed on the inevitable path He must tread. There was no panic, no bitterness, only the quiet acceptance of the Father's will and the fulfillment of prophecy. This serene acceptance lent Him an aura of strength that both comforted and contrasted starkly with the disciples' rising fear.

As the disciples grappled with the disclosure, Jesus imparted wisdom to prepare their hearts for the trial ahead. He spoke not only of betrayal but also of the cost of discipleship, exhorting them to love one another as He loved them. In this command lay a profound call to unity and forgiveness, a light piercing the encroaching darkness. It was a reminder that, even in the face of treachery, the bond forged by their Master's sacrificial love would endure beyond suffering and death.

Following the meal, moments unfolded that would etch themselves into the annals of sacred history. Jesus led His disciples to the Garden of Gethsemane, a place where olive trees whispered beneath the night sky. Here, the narrative deepens, inviting the reader into the intimate chamber of spiritual struggle and watchfulness. The atmosphere was thick with foreboding, yet it was also suffused with prayer, hope, and a palpable sense of imminent sacrifice.

Jesus's footsteps were heavy, the weight of the coming hour pressing upon Him with oppressive force. As He withdrew slightly from His disciples, His prayer took on a desperate intensity. He beseeched the Father for strength, seeking to align His own will with the divine purpose, even as the shadows of pain and death loomed ahead. "Father, if it be possible, let this cup pass from me: nevertheless not as I will, but as thou wilt." These words reveal the profound agony entwined with divine obedience, a heart torn between the desire for self-preservation and the call to redemptive love.

Meanwhile, the disciples, though instructed to watch and pray, were overcome by weariness and sleep. Their slumber amidst such a critical juncture underscores the frailty of human resolve when faced with spiritual trial. The contrast between Jesus's sleepless vigil and their drowsiness draws a poignant picture of loneliness and burden. It evokes the timeless struggle of faithfulness under duress, inviting readers to reflect on their own moments of spiritual weakness and the need for perseverance.

This night of vigil is not merely a setting for imminent betrayal and arrest; it is a profound tableau of human and divine interplay. The garden becomes a battleground where flesh, spirit, and destiny converge. Jesus's anguish and steadfastness resonate as the embodiment of sacrificial love, while the disciples' faltering watchfulness serves as a mirror to our own struggles with faith and fear.

The tension escalates as Judas approaches, his footsteps betraying the few heartbeats left before the Passion unfolds. Each flicker of torchlight, each whispered name, carries the weight of treason and sorrow. The disciples' turmoil culminates in a moment of confusion and fear, for their bond, once so secure, is rent open by betrayal's cruel hand.

Yet, even in this darkest hour, the narrative offers glimpses of hope and redemption. Jesus's prayers affirm the Father's sovereign plan; His forgiveness extends to the betrayer; His disciples are called to grow in love and courage beyond their present weakness. The night thus becomes not only a prelude to suffering but a crucible in which faith is tested and ultimately refined.

Through the finely wrought psychological portrait of this evening, readers are drawn into the complex interplay of human frailty and divine love. The dialogues, silences, and gestures breathe with emotional authenticity, making the experience vivid and immediate. It is a moment pregnant with meaning, forever echoing the tension between betrayal and fidelity, fear and faith, despair and hope.

In conclusion, "Betrayal Foretold and a Night of Vigil" captures the profound spiritual and emotional drama that marked the threshold of the Passion. It invites readers to enter the inner world of the disciples and their Lord, to feel the weight of impending tragedy, and to witness the unwavering resolve of Jesus in the face of overwhelming darkness. This subchapter serves as a vital bridge, preparing hearts for the unfolding sacrifice and the ultimate triumph of resurrection life.

The Agony in Gethsemane

The Weight of Prayer

In the solitude of the olive grove, beneath a canopy of ancient branches that stretched toward the limitless heavens, the night pressed in with a quietude so profound it seemed the very air was holding its breath. The coolness of the evening settled softly upon the earth, wrapping the landscape in a cloak of shadow and silence. The stars above flickered faintly, their distant light filtered through the darkened leaves, casting mottled patterns upon the ground. Here, in this sacred space, the trembling of a soul unfolded, the weight of prayer heavy upon the one who knelt alone.

Jesus withdrew from His disciples, whose weary forms lay scattered amid the whispering trees, their slow, irregular breaths blending into the night's symphony. The height of His burden was yet unseen by them, the gathering storm of His destiny pressing upon His heart with an oppressive force. The olive grove, known as Gethsemane, became a sanctuary and a crucible, a place where humanity and divinity met in fragile tension, where the eternal would wrestle with the temporal in the depths of prayer.

He sank to His knees upon the uneven ground, the cool soil pressing against His skin like a solemn reminder of His mortal frame. His hands found the earth beneath the trembling branches, the rough texture grounding Him in His flesh. The faint rustle of leaves overhead was the only witness to the heavy sigh that escaped His lips, labored, fragile, human. His lips, parched and cracked from days of weariness and sorrow, barely parted as a desperate plea took shape. Yet, within that plea was a surrender deeper than any resistance: "Father, if it be possible, let this cup pass from me: nevertheless not as I will, but as thou wilt."

The dryness of His lips echoed the barrenness of the moment, a silence too vast for words, too piercing to bear alone. His heart thundered within His chest, a relentless drumbeat of fear, sorrow, and resolve. It was not a quiet heartbeat; it was the kind that pounds fiercely when the soul is trembling at the edge of a great abyss. The pulse was a drum of divine agony and human weakness intertwined, a tempo that quickened with every thought of the suffering yet to come. Each beat was a message, sent from the depths of His being upward in prayer and a melody of anguish.

His hands trembled as they pressed harder against the cool earth, seeking something solid in a world that seemed suddenly uncertain. There was a rawness in those trembling fingers, an exposure of flesh and spirit that no human eye could see, but which the heavens beheld with holy sorrow. The same hands that had healed the sick, blessed the children, and calmed the storms now quivered beneath the weight of an eternal sacrifice soon to be borne.

The silence around Him was heavy with expectation yet filled with a holy loneliness. In this moment, the Son of God was fully aware of the gulf that lay between heaven and earth, between glory and suffering. His prayer echoed through the night like a fragile bridge spanning that divine chasm. It was a call and a submission; a conversation steeped in love, dread, and obedience.

The garden seemed to lean closer, the ancient olive trees bearing witness to the gravity of the moment with silent solemnity. Their gnarled limbs reached out like the arms of saints, and the leaves whispered faintly in the cool air, as if murmuring the unspoken words of heaven itself. The scent of the earth mingled with the faint fragrance of the trees, a quiet perfume carried on the night breeze, a reminder of creation standing near while creation's Redeemer wrestled with His fate.

In this place, time seemed to slow, and eternity stretched thin over the fragile heart of a man who was also God. Every breath drawn inward was a labor, every tear unshed a testament to the battle within. The agony was not only in the physical torment that awaited but in the spiritual separation, the crushing knowledge of being made sin for the world, the bearing of its brokenness alone.

His face, illuminated faintly by the starlight filtering through the branches, revealed the depths of His suffering. The furrow of His brow, the tightening of His jaw, the tremor in the muscles of His cheeks, each line a scripture of pain and resolve. Yet in these quiet moments, there was also the serene light of surrender, a radiance born of perfect trust despite profound distress.

The sacred language of prayer spilled forth, words laden with the weight of heaven and expressed through a trembling voice. It was an intimate dialogue between Father and Son, a meeting of divine wills where love embraced the necessity of sacrifice. The words carried both the burden of the coming cross and the peace that only submission to the Father's plan could bring.

His prayers were not mere utterances but the very breath of His soul made visible and audible. They bore the gravity of a covenant about to be fulfilled and the depths of a love willing to endure every agony for the redemption of mankind. Within the trembling echo of those prayers were contained the mysteries of mercy and justice intertwined, the eternal cost of grace revealed.

The agony pressed upon His spirit like waves against rock, relentless and exhausting. Each moment stretched into an eternity where pain and love fused into one. The cool night air was a sharp contrast to the burning sorrow within; the darkness of the garden a mirror to the shadow of death looming near. Yet throughout this sacred agony, a light shone, the unwavering, unyielding will to do the Father's will, no matter the cost.

The smell of crushed olive leaves filled the air, mingling with the faint sweat of His laboring flesh. The whisper of His breath, shallow and quickened, mingled with the subtle sounds of the nocturnal world around Him. These small, intimate details conveyed the fragile humanity of the Son of Man, caught in the deepest intersection of earthly pain and heavenly purpose.

The prayer continued, a sacred litany ascending from the heart of the one who bore all sin, sorrow, and shame. It was a prayer of both asking and surrendering, trembling hands lifted in trust despite the shattering weight of what lay ahead. "Abba, Father," the words began, an ancient term of intimacy and love, expressing both the closeness of their relationship and the heaviness of the cross to come.

As He prayed, His soul was cast down unto death, as the scriptures whisper. The full measure of human anguish and divine burden pressed upon Him, a weight more crushing than the stones beneath His knees. Yet through it all, amid the dryness of His mouth and the pounding of His heart, there was an unbroken thread of hope, a hope rooted in the knowledge that the purpose of this terrible hour was redemptive.

His mind recalled the tender moments of His ministry, the gentle touch of a child's hand, the healing of the blind, the feeding of the multitudes. Those memories were bittersweet now, a reminder of the love that had brought Him to this place. Each miracle, each word of mercy, was a prelude to the greatest act of love yet to be given. His prayers carried the weight not only of His own soul but of all humanity's hopes and fears.

The solitude enveloped Him, thick and profound, yet not altogether desolate. For in this loneliness lay the deepest communion with the Father, a sacred exchange far beyond what mortal words could convey. The cries of His heart poured forth in silence, unheard by human ears but amplified in heaven's throne room. It was here, in the quiet shadows of Gethsemane, that the meeting of heaven and earth reached its fullest expression.

With every pulse of His pounding heart, the decision pressed ever closer. The cup of suffering, the path of sorrow, the will to embrace the cross, all held in the fragile hands of prayer. And yet, paradoxically, in the midst of His trembling and tears, there was strength. Not the strength of power or might, but the strength born of perfect surrender and love.

The olive leaves whispered above Him, the night air breathed gently against His skin, and in the stillness His soul cried out in a harmony of agony and trust. The trembling hands, the dry lips, the pounding heart, all became the sacred vessels through which the Son of Man bore the world's weight in prayer.

As the hours deepened into the night, His prayers grew more fervent, the struggle within more intense. The disciples, though near, remained unaware of the spiritual battle unfolding just steps away. Their slumber was a stark contrast to the Son's wakefulness, a watchfulness born not only of physical sorrow but of divine mission.

In this garden, the lines between the human and the divine blurred into a sacred mystery. The vulnerability of the Son revealed the depths of His love; the weight of prayer reflected the cost of salvation. Here was the heart of Gethsemane: a profound meeting place where heaven touched earth in trembling, aching prayer.

The night air tightened like a shroud as final words passed His lips, not a resignation born of weakness but a surrender steeped in obedience and love. The cup would not pass; the will of the Father would be done, even unto death. And in that obedience lay the seed of resurrection, the dawn of eternal hope for all creation.

The weight of prayer was a burden heavier than any human could bear, yet borne with divine courage and unshakable trust. It was the silent agony of love incarnate, the intersection where the fullness of heaven met the depths of human suffering. And it was here, in the lonely olive grove, that the Son of God showed the world the true power of prayer, raw, vulnerable, desperate, yet utterly surrendered to the Father's will.

Disciples' Sleepless Weakness

As Jesus entered the Garden of Gethsemane under the weight of an impending destiny, the scene soon shifted from His solemn vigil to the fragile state of His closest companions. The disciples, those whom He had called to follow Him, to learn from Him, and to stand beside Him in the hour of trial, found themselves overcome not by spiritual strength, but by a profound human weakness. In the cherished moments meant for watchfulness and prayer, their bodies succumbed to exhaustion, their minds to weariness, and their spirits to confusion. This failing is not merely a footnote in the story of the Passion, but a poignant testament to the very real struggle of human frailty when confronted with suffering and fear.

The narrative in the Gospel of Matthew presents a vivid picture: "Watch and pray, that ye enter not into temptation: the spirit indeed is willing, but the flesh is weak" (Matt. 26:41). These words, uttered by Jesus himself, encapsulate the deep tension between intention and ability, the battle waged within each disciple's heart and body. While their spirits may have desired to be vigilant, their flesh, their mortal weakness, brought them low. This stark contrast between will and weakness unfolds amid the unfolding tragedy and strengthens the emotional gravity of the ensuing suffering.

The disciples' sleep is not simply sleep; it is a fragmented, piecemeal rest, marked more by vulnerability than by peace. They do not slumber with comfort but are found intermittently nodding off in a garden heavy with sorrow and shadow. The breaking of their watch becomes emblematic, a small yet weighty failure mirroring the looming failure that will soon come to pass at the betrayal and arrest of Jesus. Their eyes grow heavy, their limbs slacken, and their senses dull, each moment of sleep an image of human limitation faced with divine sorrow.

The Gospel accounts do not shy away from portraying the disciples in this state of exhaustion. Luke writes that Jesus found them "sleeping for sorrow" (Luke 22:45), a phrase pregnant with meaning. Their weariness is not the ordinary fatigue that follows a day's labor, but a sorrow so deep that it drains the vigor from their bodies. This sorrow is the first real taste of the burdens they carry but do not yet fully comprehend. It blends the physical tiredness of their journey and the emotional weight of the events to come, composing a portrait of fragile men struggling to grasp the severity of the moment.

Mark's Gospel provides another layer of nuance, recounting how Jesus came thrice to wake them, finding them "sleeping again, for their eyes were very heavy" (Mark 14:40). The repetition underscores their inability, not for lack of trying, but because their flesh was overwhelmed by exhaustion. Each return to wakefulness is tinged with Jesus' gentle admonition, the call to spiritual alertness that they cannot summon within their tired bodies. Their drowsiness, framed through the lens of vulnerability and burden, deepens the theme of human limitation amidst divine struggle.

John's account adds a subtle but profound insight into this dynamic by naming the disciples who accompanied Jesus into the garden Peter, James, and John. It was these three who were invited into the deeper moment of Jesus' anguish, yet even they faltered. Their failure to remain watchful is a window into the overwhelming nature of grief and fear. The closeness to Jesus does not guarantee strength; intimacy does not shield one from the weight of human frailty. Their sleep becomes a silent confession of their inability to fully bear the crisis alongside their Master.

The imagery of sleep amidst such tension also carries symbolic weight. Sleep, in biblical narrative, often represents vulnerability, a lapse in vigilance, and a susceptibility to evil or temptation. Here, it echoes the warning the disciples received, to watch and pray lest they fall into temptation. Their sleep, therefore, is not a passive state but an active surrender, a yielding to weakness that contrasts sharply with Jesus' own battle in prayer. In this contrast, the solitude of the Savior is heightened, for as they rest in fragility, He wrestles with anguish and submission.

The emotional landscape of this moment is rich with pathos. The disciples' failure is not born of cruelty or disloyalty, but of exhaustion and misunderstanding. They do not grasp the full weight of what is about to unfold, and so their prayers fail, their watchfulness fades, and their bodies betray them. This paints a deeply human scene, imperfect men caught in a divine tragedy, struggling to sustain faith and courage when the hour is darkest. Their vulnerability invites empathy rather than judgment, their weakness a mirror reflecting each reader's own moments of faltering faith.

Moreover, their sleeping forms cast a shadow upon the meaning of discipleship. To follow Christ entails more than enthusiasm or aspiration; it requires courage amid fear, steadfastness amid pain, and vigilance amid sorrow. The disciples' inability to stay awake reveals the costliness of this calling and the harsh realities of human limitation. It is a reminder that spiritual strength does not erase physical frailty and that even the closest followers can falter under pressure.

The narrative also subtly reveals the isolation inherent in Jesus' experience. Though He is surrounded by friends, their failure to watch makes His solitude more acute. The garden becomes a stage of almost solitary confrontation between Jesus and the gravity of His mission. As the disciples sleep, unaware of the full spiritual battle taking place, Jesus is left to wrestle with His foreseen suffering alone. This intensifies the sense of loneliness, the feeling that the weight of salvation rests chiefly upon the shoulders of One, while His companions are lost in sleep.

This scene also holds prophetic elements, foreshadowing the disciples' desertion and Peter's denial during the unfolding Passion. Their inability to stay awake parallels their coming spiritual failures, emphasizing the gap between human resolve and human weakness. It paints a comprehensive picture of the cost of discipleship and the price paid by Jesus and His followers alike.

In this fragile tableau, the disciples emerge not as heroic figures but as real human beings, tired, confused, sorrowful. Their physical weakness becomes a metaphor for the spiritual exhaustion that often besets believers in times of trial. It humanizes the biblical story, bridging the ancient text with the lives of readers who know the struggles of faith in moments of darkness.

The tension between the disciples' sleep and Jesus' wakefulness serves as an invitation to meditate upon the nature of prayer, watchfulness, and endurance. It challenges readers to consider their own vulnerabilities: Where do they fall asleep amid their own Gethsemanes? How do they wrestle with weakness when confronted with suffering or temptation? The disciples' failure becomes a mirror reflecting the universal human condition, caught between the spirit's willingness and the flesh's frailty.

Furthermore, this moment accentuates the paradox of divine strength paired with human weakness. In Jesus, divine strength faces the full weight of human suffering and abandonment, while in His disciples, human weakness confronts the challenge of spiritual alertness and courage. This juxtaposition is central to the Christian narrative, revealing both the necessity of divine grace and the reality of human dependence.

In understanding the disciples' sleep in Gethsemane, readers gain more than a historical insight; they receive a spiritual lesson woven into the fabric of the Passion story. It is a lesson of humility in the face of weakness, compassion for those who fail, and a deepening awareness of the necessity for prayer and reliance on God's strength. Their weakness, immortalized in the sacred text, becomes a source of comfort and identification for all who wrestle with faith and endurance.

Thus, the disciples' sleepless weakness is not merely a failure to keep watch, it is a profound moment filled with emotion, symbolism, and human truth. It deepens the narrative richness of the Agony in Gethsemane, providing a counterpoint to Jesus' steadfastness and illuminating the fragile fidelity of those He called to follow Him. Through their sleep, the story speaks across the centuries, inviting readers into a place of understanding, humility, and compassion, reminding all of the power of grace amidst human frailty.

Arrest and Quiet Resignation

The night air hung heavy over the garden of Gethsemane, cloaked in a silence broken only by the murmurs of the olive trees swaying gently in the breeze. The sacred ground, long a place of refuge and prayer, now felt the weight of an impending sorrow, as if the very earth itself trembled under the burden of what was about to unfold. It was here, beneath the shadow of ancient branches and amidst the darkness of the night, that the culmination of Jesus's earthly mission drew inexorably near.

Suddenly, the stillness was shattered. From the shadows emerged a band of men, their feet stirring the dust of the narrow paths, their presence a harsh contrast to the serenity of the garden. The sound of armor clinking lightly, of swords humming softly in their sheaths, and the murmured commands exchanged with urgency pierced the quiet like a knife. The sudden intrusion was a stark reminder that the hour of destiny had arrived.

The sounds came first, before the figures were fully revealed. The shuffling of footsteps, a low murmur of voices, and then the sharp crack of a command given in haste. The men moved deliberately, though cautious under the looming threat of discovery. Their eyes sought Him, the one they called Jesus of Nazareth, the man whose words and actions had stirred the hearts and fears of many.

Caught off guard for a moment, the disciples looked toward the gathering threat with confusion and dread. Some gripped their swords; others whispered prayers as their eyes darted between Jesus and the oncoming group. The tension was almost palpable. It was not simply the sense of danger that gripped them but the deep sorrow that shadowed their understanding of what this arrest meant.

Then He came forth, stepping silently into the lantern light that flickered against the trembling leaves. His face, soft and serene, held no hallmarks of fear or resistance. In that moment, the stark contrast between His calm and the storm of emotions roiling within His companions was overwhelming. There was a heaviness in His gaze, a quiet resignation that spoke volumes beyond the need for spoken words.

The cold grasp of capture was swift. Hands, rough and determined, reached out, encircling Him with a restraint that betrayed a mixture of urgency and reverence. Yet even as the soldiers took hold, Jesus did not flinch nor resist. The very calmness of His acceptance seemed to still the air itself, freezing the frantic energy of the night into a solemn tableau.

"Whom seek ye?" He asked, His voice steady, carrying across the tense silence like a beacon.

"Jesus of Nazareth," was the reply.

"I am He," He answered.

Upon hearing this, those who had come to take Him stepped backward, staggered as if struck. There was an unspoken power in those words, an authority untouched by the looming threat of violence. The glow from the torches reflected in the eyes of the men, some filled with uncertainty, others steeled with duty, as the mystery of who stood before them deepened.

In the midst of this, a betrayal pierced the night: the kiss of Judas. A seemingly tender gesture, yet one loaded with consequence, it marked the precise moment when the divine plan moved into the realm of human hands and frailty. Judas approached, his lips touching Jesus's cheek, an act deceptive in its tenderness, yet unmistakable in its intent. Jesus met his traitorous friend with neither anger nor rebuke. Instead, there was a profound sadness that seemed to echo across the garden, intertwining with the rustling leaves and whispered prayers.

The soldiers moved quickly, securing Jesus with cords and preparing to lead Him away from the sanctuary of Gethsemane and into the night that would bear witness to His passion. His disciples, overwhelmed by fear and sorrow, scattered into the shadows, their hearts breaking as they watched the man who had given them hope now under guard, defenseless yet unbowed.

Through this chaos, Jesus carried Himself with a dignity unshaken by His physical capture. There was a lesson in His quiet acceptance, a surrender not born of weakness but of resolute obedience to the will of His Father. Each step He took into the night was heavy with the weight of the world's sins, yet lightened by the certainty of purpose.

The sounds of the garden faded as He was led away, the crunch of feet on gravel, the soft murmur of voices, the distant call of a night bird. The world around Him seemed unaware or indifferent to the momentous event unfolding within its midst. Yet the heavens bore witness in silent testament, and the earth beneath seemed to shudder at the loss of its Redeemer.

There, in that hush before the dawn, sorrow and resolve entwined themselves around the heart of the universe. A sorrow born of betrayal, abandonment, and the impending suffering that would soon consume the Son of God. And yet, intertwined with that sorrow, a resolve unmatched, an endurance fortified by divine love and unyielding faith.

The night did not seize the final word. It was merely the beginning of the passage, a gateway through which He would walk alone to the cross, to death, and ultimately to resurrection. The quiet resignation that filled Jesus in that dark hour was not defeat but acceptance, an acceptance that carried with it the promise of redemption for all mankind.

As the men led Him away from Gethsemane, the garden returned to its silence, but the echoes of what transpired lingered, imprinting themselves upon the very soul of creation. The calm before the storm had given way to a new chapter in the divine story, charged with grief, yet bursting with hope. The arrest was a somber reminder of the cost of salvation, and the steady, unshaken posture of Jesus in the midst of turmoil revealed a profound strength, inviting all who witnessed to behold the depth of His love.

And so the narrative moves forward, from the quiet garden to the courts of judgment, the mocking crowds, and the hill called Calvary. The Passion of Christ, though marked by suffering and death, is underscored by this moment of quiet resignation, where surrender without resistance reveals the power of divine love and foreshadows the triumph that would echo through eternity.

The Passion: A Passionate Portrait

Trials Before Pilate and the Crowds

The morning light filtered weakly through the narrow windows of the praetorium, casting long shadows across the cold stone floors. The air hung heavy with tension, thick enough that every breath seemed measured and deliberate. Pilate, the Roman governor, sat upon his raised judgment seat, his robes rustling softly as he adjusted his posture to face the growing crowd beyond the courtyard. The faint echo of footsteps reverberated off the hard stones, the restless movements of soldiers, servants, and the assembled Jewish leaders, each playing a part in the unfolding drama.

Inside the chamber, an oppressive stillness bore down on all present. Yet beyond the walls, voices rose and fell like a tempest. The murmurs, first whispers and swells of agitation, now melded into clamorous cries demanding judgment. Pilate's gaze lingered over the gathering throng of accusers arrayed before him. Their faces were fiery with zeal, eyes ablaze with condemnation but betraying unease beneath the surface. It was not mere anger that propelled them but a complicated web of fear, envy, and the inexorable force of religious law.

The man who stood accused, Jesus of Nazareth, appeared composed, his countenance unmarred by the noise and fury surrounding him. He was a figure of calm amidst the storm, his eyes unblinking, meeting Pilate's gaze without fear or evasion. In his silence, there was a weight that pressed upon the crowd, a gravity that unsettled some and intrigued others. His presence itself seemed to challenge the very proceedings, as if the heavenly and earthly courts had collided in this dimly lit hall.

Pilate's disposition was conflicted. His experience as a Roman magistrate had honed his instincts for maintaining order and showcasing imperial power, yet here he faced a case that transcended simple law enforcement. Accused of rebellion and blasphemy, Jesus posed a conundrum: a man reportedly claiming kingship but showing no weapons, no armies, no means to usurp Roman rule. The governor's mind churned, attempting to disentangle truths buried beneath the layers of accusation, political maneuvering, and religious fervor.

The charges leveled against Jesus were grave and multifaceted. The Jewish leaders declared that He threatened to overthrow Caesar's authority by proclaiming Himself King of the Jews, a direct political challenge that demanded swift Roman reprisal. Yet when Pilate interrogated Jesus, he found no clear admission of sedition. The prisoner's words were measured, almost enigmatic. "My kingdom is not of this world," Jesus declared softly, his voice cutting through the cacophony like a blade. This statement perplexed Pilate, for it hinted at a reign beyond earthly dominion, a divine kingship that man's courts could neither comprehend nor adjudicate.

As the questioning continued, the atmosphere grew more charged. The stone floor beneath Pilate seemed to resonate with the escalating tension, footsteps pounding rhythmically as cohorts of priests and elders pushed forward with their complaints. Their voices crescendoed, "Crucify him! Crucify him!" The repeated chant became a relentless drumbeat echoing through the corridors. Each call for death chipped away at the air, suffocating any attempt at reasoned debate or mercy.

Pilate's countenance betrayed his inner turmoil. The weight of governance pressed upon him, the scales tipping precariously between justice and political expediency. Jewish customs and Roman law clashed like thunder overhead, and the governor feared unrest that might spiral beyond his control. He sought to absolve himself, publicly washing his hands to symbolize his claimed innocence over the fate about to unfold. Yet no act of symbol or word could erase the knowledge that power was being wielded to sacrifice innocence.

The crowds, a volatile sea of emotion, held power of their own. Fueled by leaders who stirred their passions, they demanded swift and final judgment. Their voices rumbled with accusations that seemed both rehearsed and visceral: false charges of treason, blasphemy, and rebellion. Yet beneath the surface, some faces showed doubt, others sorrow, and many just the blankness of submission. The mass was both a force of nature and a mirror to human frailty, easily swayed, quick to condemn, yet capable of fleeting compassion caught in the undercurrent.

Amidst this chaos, silence descended sporadically, a pregnant pause in the tempest, allowing the gravity of events to settle, however briefly. In these quiet moments, Pilate searched the prisoner's eyes, seeking a sign, a confession, a plea that might tip the scales. Jesus offered none. Instead, He spoke of truths eternal, of kingdoms not bound by earth's corruptions, and of a destiny foretold beyond human reckoning. His words were neither defense nor denial but an invitation to perceive a greater narrative in which both judge and accused were mere actors.

The judicial process itself became a theater where cosmic forces converged. Pilate, the embodiment of imperial power, performed his role with all outward authority, yet his conscience was ensnared by something beyond political survival. The Jewish leaders wielded religious authority and tradition but masked their fear of losing control amid an increasingly restless populace. The crowd, human and unpredictable, swayed like reeds in the wind, carried by songs and shouts that obscured truth and justice.

False accusations were hurled with fervent conviction. Witnesses stepped forward with contradictory testimonies, their words crafted to ensnare rather than illuminate. The cacophony of claims and counterclaims crafted a labyrinth of deception and partial truths. Inside the sanctity of the trial hall, whispers collided with cries, and the sense of impending doom thickened the atmosphere. Every breath inhaled was heavy with betrayal; every step taken echoed the approaching darkest hour.

Pilate wrestled with his prerogative as judge and the demands of political pragmatism. He sought to release Jesus, offering the crowd a choice between the condemned man and Barabbas, a known insurrectionist. Yet the tumultuous crowd rejected clemency, their chosen champion stained with bloodshed. This refusal illuminated the deeper tragedy, justice perverted, innocence forsaken for the sake of placating unrest and preserving fragile power.

The final moments before sentencing were marked by an uneasy stillness pierced by sporadic cries. Pilate, in an act of resignation and cynicism, declared, "I am innocent of the blood of this just person: see ye to it." With those words, responsibility was cast like a shadow onto the crowd, yet the inevitable was sealed. The governor's internal conflict remained unresolved, a testament to the collision of human governance and divine purpose.

As Jesus was led away to the place of crucifixion, the echoes of the trial lingered, stone floors still cold beneath pounding boots, murmurs of conspiracy seeping into the stones, the silence between shouts pregnant with unspeakable sorrow. This moment encapsulated a paradox: the weight of human injustice intertwined with the unfolding of a divine plan that would forever alter the course of history.

The trial before Pilate was more than a mere legal proceeding: it was a nexus where political calculation, religious fervor, and eternal destiny converged. It revealed the frailty and complexity of humanity, the capacity for cruelty masked by law, the thirst for power cloaked in righteousness, and the profound mystery of redemptive sacrifice played out on an earthly stage. The stones themselves, worn and unmoved, bore silent witness to this solemn intersection of time, law, and the eternal will of God.

Every detail, the echo of footsteps down cold stone halls, the murmured conspiracies among the priests, the seething shouts of the crowd drowning out justice, painted a portrait of a world caught between darkness and the dawning light of salvation. The trial's narrative tension serves not only to chronicle events but to invite reflection on the profound human and cosmic significance embodied by Jesus of Nazareth, condemned by men but destined to reign forevermore.

Mockery and Scourging

The scene of mockery and scourging that Jesus endured before His crucifixion stands as one of the most harrowing moments of His Passion, a moment heavy with both physical agony and profound emotional torment. The King James Bible recounts these events with stark clarity, unveiling a vivid tableau of cruelty and humiliation that invites us to witness the full depth of Jesus's suffering. To fully appreciate the gravity of this ordeal, we must set ourselves before the scene with attentive hearts and open minds, allowing the sensory details and emotional contrasts to speak afresh to our understanding.

As Jesus was led away to be judged by Pontius Pilate, the weight of His impending sacrifice began to press visibly upon His shoulders. The scourging was not merely a punishment but a preparation, a brutal greeting to the cross. The Roman scourge, known for its merciless composition of leather thongs tipped with sharp pieces of bone or metal, was designed to tear flesh openly and painfully. The lashes fell with furious and unrelenting force, each strike awakening the raw nerve endings beneath His skin, rending muscle and drawing free blood. Imagining this scene, one feels the sting of the lashes, the wet warmth of blood mingling with dust and sweat, coating the ground beneath Him.

The biblical text tells us that Jesus was subjected to this scourging without resistance or complaint, revealing a dignity that transcended the immediate torment. The severity of the scourging was such that the flesh upon His back was torn to the point of exposure, a writhing canvas painting the price of salvation in crimson strokes. The physical suffering was compounded by the emotional weight of isolation and humiliation. To be scourged publicly, stripped of His dignity and exposed as a common criminal, was to suffer not only pain of body but of soul. Yet, even within this intense scene of agony, Jesus maintained a divine composure, a silent acceptance and forgiveness that stood in stark contrast to the cruelty inflicted upon Him.

This endurance invites readers into a profound empathetic connection; through the sensory recollection of the stinging lashes and the sight of bloodied flesh, we glimpse the magnitude of His sacrifice. The dust beneath His feet, stained with His blood, becomes emblematic of the burden borne for humanity, while the gray, somber sky suspends the moment in an eternal stillness, as if creation itself mourned the pain unfolding beneath.

Following the scourging came the intensification of mockery, a psychological torture designed to compound Jesus's physical suffering with scorn and degradation. The soldiers, having stripped Him of His garments, clothed Him in a robe of scarlet, intended as a cruel mimicry of royal vestments. Upon His head, they placed a crown of thorn branches, piercing His scalp with angry, unforgiving points. These thorns, digging deep into His flesh, added sharp, relentless pain to the open wounds already etched across His back. The sight of this crowned "king" was an unbearable insult, a bitter caricature of honor and power.

The soldiers then mocked Him with derisive salutes, bending their knees before Him in false homage while spitting and striking Him. Their words, laced with sarcasm and contempt, sought to break His spirit, but He endured in silent strength. This scene unfolds like a cruel theater in which Jesus is both the victim and the unwilling actor, bearing the full weight of human scorn for a purpose far greater than the derision of His tormentors. The contrast between the brutality of their actions and the immovable calm of His countenance serves as a profound testament to His inner resolve.

Sensory details continue to enrich this narrative, inviting readers to sense the rough pressure of the wooden staff thrust into His back, the prickling sting of thorns, the metallic taste of blood mingling with dust in His mouth. The soldiers' voices echo like thunder in the mind, harsh, mocking, yet hollow, unable to touch the deep dignity that remains unbroken. The scene is painted in bold strokes: the red blood against pale flesh, the vibrant scarlet robe against somber earth tones, the sharp contrast of jagged thorns against soft skin.

This moment of mockery and scourging is more than a mere historical account; it is a carefully preserved spiritual witness that draws readers into the heart of the Passion. The emotional dimension is enriched by the interplay between unyielding cruelty and an enduring grace that cannot be diminished. In this interplay, a sacred intimacy is forged. We do not merely observe Jesus's suffering from afar; rather, we are invited to enter into it, to feel the lashes, to hear the jeers, and to understand the depth of His sacrifice in a manner both visceral and profound.

The gray sky overhead, an almost tangible presence in the scene, seems to absorb the pain and sorrow, mirroring the heaviness that weighed not only upon Jesus but upon all creation at that time. It is under this somber canopy that the full spectacle of His mockery unfolds, not as spectacle for amusement, but as a sacred drama that echoes through eternity. The mingling of blood and dust underfoot becomes a silent witness to the cost of redemption, a reminder that every humiliation, every tear, every scar was borne willingly for the salvation of mankind.

In reflecting upon this scene, one cannot help but be drawn into a deeper contemplation of what such suffering entails. The scourging broke the body; the mockery sought to break the spirit. Yet neither succeeded. The steadfastness of Jesus in the face of such overwhelming adversity becomes a beacon for believers, a powerful example of perseverance and love. The vivid imagery of this moment ensures that the story of His Passion is not an abstract theological concept but a lived experience, tangible and accessible to those who seek to understand.

By engaging with these details, the sting of each lash, the sharp bite of thorns, the weight of derision, we come to understand more fully the magnitude of Jesus's sacrifice. It was a suffering that encompassed the whole human experience: physical pain, emotional agony, and social rejection. Yet through it all shone a dignity and divine grace that transformed pain into love, humiliation into glory. This paradox lies at the heart of the Passion narrative and invites readers into a deeper appreciation of the mystery of the cross.

Thus, the episode of mockery and scourging is not merely a painful interlude before the crucifixion; it is a revelation of the depth of divine compassion, the cost of redemption, and the triumph of gracious endurance over vileness. It calls us to remember with reverence the intensity of Jesus's suffering and to respond with hearts full of gratitude and faith. Through the vivid and respectful retelling of this scene, the narrative fosters an intimate bond between the reader and the Savior, one that transcends time and space and continues to resonate with profound spiritual power.

The Way of the Cross

The procession toward Golgotha unfolded beneath a sky burdened with heavy clouds, as though the heavens themselves mourned the ordeal about to be endured. The air hung thick with a weight beyond the mere physical strains of the day, a profound sadness that seemed to seep into every heart and stone along the narrow road leading out of Jerusalem. Jesus, clad now in the rough garment that mocked His kingship, moved steadily, each step a deliberate act of will, a testimony to the profound purpose that bore Him onward despite the agony already etched deep into His body.

The journey from the praetorium out to the site of crucifixion was no simple passage but a crucible of suffering that encompassed both the physical and the spiritual realms. The friction between flesh and burden manifested in the relentless pressure of the crossbeam pressing against Jesus's shoulders, slicing into His already bruised skin with each labored step. His muscles, once robust and full of life, now trembled beneath the crushing weight, sinews tightening to endure the unyielding pain. The wood was coarse and unyielding, the roughness scraping against His torn flesh, reminding all who looked on that this journey was cruelly designed to break the body as well as the spirit.

Despite the toll on His frame, Jesus pressed forward, not with the desperation of defeat but with the quiet resolve of one who embraced the path laid before Him. His eyes, though swollen and shadowed with weariness, cast glances not of anger or despair, but of compassion. Amid the jeers of the hostile crowds and the severity of the Roman soldiers' commands, there was a gaze that caught the look of the weeping women, the humble followers who dared to walk alongside Him in sorrowful sympathy. In these moments, Jesus's internal landscape was a battlefield not solely of physical endurance but of spiritual continuity and love.

The scene was alive with contrasts and tensions. The shouts and taunts from some sides were met with the silence of others, whose faces bore anguish and tears. Bystanders, some hidden behind hastening feet and others brave enough to meet His eyes, were drawn into the unfolding drama. The air resonated not merely with human voices but with a deeper lament that transcended mortal understanding, a cosmic sorrow reverberating through every quaking leaf, every trembling stone by the roadside.

As the procession advanced, the heavens themselves seemed to respond. Darkened skies gathered above, shadows lengthening across the path as if night sought to hasten the coming of the end. The light wavered uncertainly, as if the very source of daylight recoiled from the weight of what was transpiring beneath it. Occasional tremors ran through the earth, subtle yet undeniable. The ground bore witness to a tragedy greater than any human injustice, the very foundation of the world trembling under the grief and gravity of the moment.

Every step forward was a verse in the silent psalm of sacrifice. The physical agony was matched by an internal fortitude that refused to falter. Jesus's mind moved beyond His own pain, extending mercy even toward those who condemned Him. The divine paradox was unmistakable: in the midst of suffering inflicted by human cruelty, He preserved compassion, praying even for the forgiveness of His executioners. His heart beat not for retribution but for redemption, a truth that illuminated the path as surely as any torch.

The weight of the crossbeam altered not just His gait but His posture, bending His frame into a silhouette of burden and surrender. Yet beneath this visible submission lay an indomitable spirit, an unshakable anchor of faith and love in the depths of adversity. The silence between the clamor of footsteps and jeers was filled with unspoken prayers, a sacred dialogue between the suffering Messiah and His Father.

The crowds formed a tapestry of humanity, the scornful, the curious, the brokenhearted, each drawn into this singular moment of divine-human intersection. Among them, Simon of Cyrene was compelled by the Roman guards to share in the burden, an unwitting participant in the unfolding drama whose own life would be forever marked by this encounter. His hands grasped the heavy beam, offering a flicker of relief to the one who bore the sins of the world, yet this act also signaled the passing of the weight to the world's conscience.

As the procession neared Golgotha, the atmosphere thickened with expectancy and dread. The hill that awaited was known as the Place of the Skull, a name steeped in foreboding yet about to be transformed by the mystery of grace. The ground here was barren and scarred, mirroring the desolation of the path taken. Every step onto this grim ascent was a step deeper into the fulfillment of ancient prophecies and eternal promises.

In these final moments before the crucifixion, time seemed both compressed and elongated. The earthly clock ticked insistently forward even as each second stretched under the weight of immeasurable significance. His breathing, uneven and ragged, was a metronome marking the slow agony of approaching sacrifice. Yet His resolve was unwavering; Jesus embraced the cross not merely as an instrument of death but as a bridge to salvation.

The narrative rhythm of this journey ebbed and flowed, sometimes a harsh cadence of laborious steps and shouted commands, sometimes falling into a softer, more reflective pace as the crowd's clamor gave way to whispered prayers and stifled sobs. The juxtaposition of noise and silence, movement and stillness, echoed the spiritual conflict that played out within Jesus's soul and resonated across creation.

Darkness began to descend prematurely, a veil of night shrouding the landscape even as the sun should have been at its zenith. This unnatural dimming was a harbinger, a signpost pointing toward the cosmic unraveling wrought by sin being borne upon this cross. The lamentations of the earth itself seemed a mournful hymn, joined by the wailing of women and the tremulous gasps of disciples overcome with sorrow.

Yet amid the grim tableaux of suffering and condemnation, there was light, a beacon of hope and divine love burning quietly within Jesus's heart. His compassion did not waver; His prayers for forgiveness and the salvation of souls reached out beyond the immediate horror, beyond the jeering crowd, to embrace the whole of humanity. Each step was a testament not only to human endurance but to divine mercy incarnate.

The procession concluded as the weary figure ascended Golgotha's rise, the summit destined to be etched forever in spiritual memory. The cross was lifted high, the nails poised to seal the ultimate covenant of love and sacrifice. The earth groaned beneath this profound act, heavens trembling as the Redeemer's mission reached its climax.

In contemplating the Way of the Cross, one is invited to witness more than suffering; one is drawn into the heart of divine resolve, into a journey marked by love that transcends torment. It is a path that calls forth our own response, a contemplation of sacrifice, mercy, and the boundless grace that flows from a God who stoops to redeem the fallen.

Thus, the Way of the Cross is not merely a physical procession but a spiritual odyssey, where each moment beats with eternal significance. It invites us to walk alongside that straining, burdened figure; to feel the weight; to hear the distant wails; to behold the darkened skies and trembling earth, and, within it all, to find a wellspring of hope and compassion that will forever illuminate the shadowed path before us.

The Silence of the Tomb

The Burial and the Heavy Stone

The day had grown dimmer as the sun retreated beneath the horizon, casting long shadows across the rocky landscape surrounding Jerusalem. The city buzzed faintly with the noise of evening preparations, yet in the garden where the tomb awaited, an unusual stillness had settled. This was a stillness woven from sorrow and gravity, a hush that seemed to stretch beyond mere silence and pressed against the very stone. It was beneath this heavy quiet that the body of Jesus of Nazareth was prepared for burial, wrapped carefully and laid to rest.

The air was thick with the mingling scents of spices and death, frankincense, myrrh, and aloes blended into a fragrant shroud that sought to both honor and preserve. The hands that tended to Jesus's body moved with purpose and tenderness; rough fingers carried the weight of grief, yet there was a reverence that transcended pain, a consciousness of the sacredness in these final acts. The linen cloth, fine and gleaming white, was laid smoothly over His form, each fold deliberate and respectful. The fabric traced the dimensions of His lifeless frame, the gentle rise and fall of muscles now stilled, the imprint of nail marks on hands and feet, the bruising and wounds that testified silently of the torment endured. This was no ordinary burial; this was the placing of the Messiah, the One who had healed, taught, and loved.

Nearby, the tomb itself awaited, a cave hewn from solid rock, its mouth barred by a heavy stone. The walls inside were cold and rugged to the touch, jagged surfaces worn unevenly by the tools of earlier labor. A faint mustiness lingered in the enclosed space, intertwined with the earthy scent of dried moss and limestone. The air was stifling, yet in this narrow chamber, where no breath stirred but the slow exhalations of the earth itself, there stood a profound quiet, a silence that pressed down like dust settling upon every surface, thick and untouchable.

Those present, the women who had followed Jesus faithfully, Joseph of Arimathea, who had requested the body, and Nicodemus, to whom the laws and customs bore a heavy weight, all moved deliberately in this time of reverence. Their eyes, softened by sorrow, gazed upon the lifeless form with a mixture of disbelief and love. The sadness was palpable, yet beneath it, there was an undercurrent of something more elusive, something veiled in mystery. The death that had claimed this man, who had been the light to so many, bore the shadow of divine purpose. It was a silence not only of absence but of waiting.

The cold stone, immense and unyielding, was rolled into place with great effort. Its weight reverberated through the ground as it settled against the tomb's entrance, sealing away the body from sight and touch. The graveyard grew darker, the last slivers of daylight filtering through cracks in the rock, casting shapes like ancient fingers reaching across the floor of the tomb. These shadows moved slowly, merging and stretching, as if mourning the presence now gone. The atmosphere felt dense with the solemnity of mortality, yet beneath the surface lay an unspoken promise, a sacred anticipation held fast in the heart of stillness.

To enter fully into the silence of this tomb is to confront the reality of death's finality. The breath that once quickened in the breath of life now hung suspended, leaving only the memory of warmth and the echo of a voice that had spoken of hope and salvation. It was a silence that spoke its own language, the language of loss made palpable, of grief etched in the roughness of stone and linen, of a heart suspended between despair and hope. The textures encountered here, the grit of dust beneath the feet, the hardness of rock, the softness of folded cloth, invite the mind to dwell on the mystery laid bare.

Yet, within this somber stillness, there rests the profound tension of divine intervention poised to shatter the bonds of death itself. The stone, though heavy and unyielding, cannot enclose the expanse of the eternal. The darkness, though thick and pressing, cannot overcome the light that had walked among men. Here, in the quiet grave, the divine promise brews silently, an unfathomable anticipation that calls the faithful to wait with patient hearts.

As the last hands withdrew from the tomb, the garden's quiet returned, enveloping all in a cold embrace. No sound disturbed the resting place save for the distant murmur of the city and the soft rustling of the olive branches overhead. The air hung motionless, save for the faintest stirrings of the nighttime breeze. This was the solemn solitude of death's shadow, where the world seemed to hold its breath.

In this moment, the very earth seemed to mourn, as though creation itself lamented the loss it had witnessed. The very stones might have remembered the heavens darkened, the veil of the temple torn, and the cry of the forsaken on the cross. The silence of the tomb stands as a counterpoint to the tumultuous passion that had preceded it, a sacred pause, a solemn interlude marked by stillness and a heavy stone.

Those who entered this place, be they mourning followers or guards stationed to prevent theft, found themselves caught in the weight of this scene, hearts humbled, spirits subdued. To touch the roughness of the stone, to trace the firmness of the linen wrappings, to breathe the thick, scented air was to step into the deepest resonance of human grief and divine mystery intertwined. The burial was not merely an act of closure but a moment pregnant with the hidden life yet to burst forth.

Here, in the cavernous dark, the narrative finds its quietest yet most profound chapter. The body lies wrapped and sealed, the world holding vigil over the lifeless form that had transformed many lives.

The heaviness of the stone mirrors the heaviness felt in the soul, a weight of separation, of grief, of the cruel finality of death. Yet that weight is also the mass against which the resurrection's force will grapple, a portent of the miraculous dawn soon to break the black silence and call forth new life.

As the night deepened, the garden sank into shadows almost complete, and the tomb itself became a sealed sanctum, untouched and inviolate. Yet beneath this outer sepulcher, an unseen power was at work, a divine stir in the stillness, a quiet deformation of death's dominion. The cold stone, the coarse walls, the fragrant linen, these were the signposts of a story reaching its deepest point, poised on the edge of the impossible.

Thus, the burial beneath the heavy stone invites reflection on the essence of death, the reverence in farewell, and the quiet anticipation of resurrection's triumph. It calls the reader into the depths of somber silence, to feel the textures of loss and the promise that waits unseen. It is here, in the grave's dark embrace, that the tension between despair and hope is most profoundly lived, and where the sacred mystery of Jesus's triumph begins to take breath.

Grief and Vigil: The Followers' Watch

In the deep, somber hush that veiled the hours following the crucifixion, a tapestry of grief and vigil unfurled around the tomb where the body of Jesus had been laid. The stone sealed the entrance like a silent sentinel guarding the heavy secret of death, yet outside, a different silence reigned, one imbued with sorrow, breathless expectation, and an aching emptiness that pressed upon the hearts of those who loved Him. This silence was not empty; it was pregnant with unspoken suffering and fragile hope.

Mary Magdalene sat apart from the others, her form fragile yet resolute in the dim light that threaded through the olive trees. The weight of grief sat heavily upon her shoulders, a shadow that dulled the vibrant light that once danced in her eyes. She, who had once known joy in Jesus' presence, now bore the crushing absence of His voice, His touch, His life. Every breath she drew seemed to echo the sorrow that gripped her soul, each sob a silent plea rising to the heavens. Her hair, once meticulously arranged, tangled and wild from days spent weeping, was a testament to nights filled with restless sorrow.

Nearby, Mary, the mother of Jesus, wept quietly, her face etched with lines of profound anguish and maternal love. Her eyes, so often filled with a quiet, steadfast faith, were now pools of tear-streaked grief. The cold night air did little to still the warmth of her tears, which ran freely down her cheeks, mingling with the dust and sweat of the day's torment. She remembered the infant He once was, the child she had held close through years of humble life, now cold and motionless in the tomb. Her hands, wrinkled and trembling, clasped a worn cloth to her breast, a small comfort against the vast void left in her heart.

The disciples, scattered and silent, found themselves actors in a terrible play whose script they could neither understand nor accept. Peter sat apart in the shadows, his face obscured, knotted fists pressed to his mouth as if to choke back the thunderous questions and bitter despair storming within him. Thomas paced in restless circles, his mind a tempest of doubt and fear. They had followed Jesus with unwavering faith, witnessed His miracles, and heard His teachings, yet now, confronted by the cruel finality of the cross, their spirits wavered. They gathered in small clusters and then fell silent, caught in the fragile web between hope and surrender.

Throughout the night, whispered prayers emerged, a murmured litany of devotion and despair mingled. Occasionally, one voice would rise above the others, trembling with broken faith, only to be swallowed by the suffocating silence once more. The prayers were not loud; they were delicate threads of sound, fragile attempts to hold on to hope when all seemed lost. "Lord, if Thou art with us still... if Thy love endures beyond this grief..." The words drifted into the cold air, hesitant and fragile.

Outside this circle of sorrow, the Roman guards maintained their grim watch. Their faces were stoic, veins taut beneath their weathered skin as they stood sentinel by the tomb's sealed stone. These were men accustomed to violence and death, yet even they were unsettled by the oppressive quiet. No laughter, no song, no sign of life stirred in the night; only the silent tomb and the shadow of a God-man whose death had shaken a city. Their eyes, sharp and watchful, scanned the darkness, each breath visible in the chill air, each moment stretching endlessly.

The guards' vigilant stance was as much burdened by fear as by duty. Deep within their chests, where duty warred with an inexplicable unease, they sensed the weight of a story far greater than a mere crucifixion. Rumors of resurrection and divine power whispered among the people, tales that defied their rational minds. They gripped the cold weapons at their sides, feeling the strange stillness press upon them, a quiet that seemed to hold its own breath, awaiting the breaking of a dawn they dared not yet hope for.

The garden surrounding the tomb bore witness to the vigil, its familiar scents transformed by the night. The fragrance of olive and myrrh mingled with the sharp tang of sweat and tears. The earth itself seemed to hold its breath, heavy and silent beneath the watchful stars. The cool breeze whispered through the trees, carrying with it the soft rustle of leaves and the distant murmur of water from a nearby spring. It was a symphony of stillness, of nature muted in reverence or dread; a world waiting, suspended between life and death.

Within the hearts of those who mourned, a trembling hope flickered, delicate and fragile, yet persistent. It was the memory of Jesus' words, spoken softly amidst crowds and whispered to His closest friends: "I am the resurrection and the life." These words, once so radiant with promise, now quivered on the edge of disbelief and longing. Beneath the veil of grief, a small, fierce ember of faith refused to be extinguished. It was a hope that perhaps, beyond the sealed stone, beyond the darkness of the tomb, life awaited.

Mary Magdalene, still seated on a cold stone, whispered a prayer thick with emotion: "If Thou hast taken Him away, tell me where Thou hast laid Him." Her voice cracked, the desperate plea a raw thread stretched across the silent night. She felt the roughness of the earth beneath her fingers, the coolness of the marble rim of the tomb, as though seeking tangible evidence that her Lord was truly gone. Yet even in her despair, her heart clung to the possibility that this was not the end.

Mary's mother's prayers were quieter, yet no less urgent. Her faith, tempered by a lifetime of trials and love, spoke in a gentle, persistent voice. "Lord, grant us peace beyond sorrow. Let Thy will, though hard to bear, be done." Her tears fell in a steady stream, mingling with the faint dew upon her garments. Her gaze lifted toward the stars, as if seeking a sign, a comfort, a message from the heavens that her son's story did not close in darkness.

Among the disciples, Peter's grief was a tempest of regret and broken resolve. He remembered his denial, the bitter words that had driven a wedge between him and his Master. Now, watching the quiet vigil, he wrestled with the ghosts of his fears and the hope that he might one day see Jesus again. The silence pressed down heavily upon him, a weight as suffocating as the night itself. Yet even amid the shadows of failure, Peter's heart stirred with a longing for redemption.

Thomas, ever the skeptic, paced with restless energy, grappling with the impossible. His mind rejected the finality of death, even as his eyes beheld the evidence of loss. He whispered pleas not just to God, but to his own reason: "Show me the way, confirm the truth, dispel the darkness." His doubts waged war against his growing desire for faith, setting his spirit at odds with itself through the weary hours.

The other disciples and followers mingled in smaller groups along the edges of the garden, each wrestling with grief in their own way. Some knelt in silent prayer, hands clenched tightly, faces buried in the dust. Others sat motionless, staring blindly into the shadowed hollow of the tomb. Mothers clutched their children close, fearful to let go, as if the life of Jesus suffused them still. Silent tears and trembling sighs wove a mournful chorus that rippled through the gathering.

Amid these scenes of raw human sorrow, a certain sacredness took hold. The vigil was more than mourning; it was an act of faith born from love, a refusal to abandon the One who had transformed their lives. In the oppressive stillness, the followers' hearts beat in tandem, each pulse a silent vow to trust beyond what they could see or understand. Even as despair threatened to engulf them, their presence at the tomb was a testimony that hope, however faint, endured.

The Roman guards, too, faced their own inner conflicts. Each shift of the night deepened the fog of unease pressing upon their consciousness. Shadows lengthened and twisted, the darkness playing tricks upon their weary minds. Some cast furtive glances toward the sealed stone, while others muttered names and phrases they barely understood, a prayer or curse, mingled with superstition. The air around them seemed thick with expectancy and fear, as if the night itself awaited a revelation.

The overseer of the guard paced beside the tomb, his armor clinking softly in the silence. His eyes, sharp but weary, scanned the horizon, looking for signs of intrusion or disturbance. Yet what troubled him most was the eerie quiet, the absence of all that once marked life in this place. A storm of questions twisted within him: Who was this man, whose death had shaken the very foundations of power and law? Could there be truth in the rumors that He was more than mortal, that His death was but a threshold to greater things? But duty bound him, and so he remained vigilant, a solitary figure in the night's lonely tableau.

The garden around the tomb remained cloaked in silence, the natural world seemingly attuned to the gravity of the moment. Crickets ceased their song; the wind softened to a breath. The olive trees stood like solemn watchers, their gnarled branches casting ghostly shadows on stones worn smooth by centuries. Here, in this sacred enclosure, time seemed to ebb, a space where the ordinary world paused to honor a mystery beyond comprehension.

Throughout these long hours, the emotional landscape of the followers was one of profound complexity. Despair hung heavily, a dark cloud that seemed ever poised to snuff out the fragile light within. Yet beneath that grief, beneath the hollow ache and tear-streaked faces, hope flickered, trembling, hesitant, unyielding. It whispered that death was not the final word, that love could transcend even the cold tomb. This hope was a seed planted deep within hearts battered by sorrow, nurtured by faith and remembrance.

As the first faint light of dawn began to stir in the east, that heavy night of vigil and grief remained etched in the memory of all who waited. The silence of the tomb had become, paradoxically, a sacred space of watchfulness and expectancy, a moment suspended in time where sorrow met faith, and despair bowed before an unseen hope.

In those fragile hours of watching and waiting, the followers of Jesus stood at the crossroads of history, caught between the shadow of death and the promise of resurrection. Their grief was real and piercing, yet within it, the quiet will to believe whispered that the story was far from over. The watch continued, not merely out of duty, but out of a love that death could not diminish, a faith that tremblingly awaited the breaking of the dawn.

The World in Waiting

Beneath a vault of midnight velvet, the stars hung like silent sentinels, their light veiled by the shroud of an event long anticipated yet not fully comprehended. The heavens, usually ablaze with the chorus of celestial fire, bore a muted glow, as if the very cosmos had drawn a breath and held it, awaiting the hour that would rend the fabric of time and space. This moment, this suspension of existence itself, was neither the end nor the beginning, but a trembling precipice between both, where the ordinary flow of days and nights hung still in a sacred pause.

The earth beneath, too, seemed to partake in this solemn silence. The fields rested under the weight of a deep hush, and the rivers mirrored a stillness so profound it was almost tangible. The birds stilled their songs, their wings folding in quiet expectation, while the trees, ancient witnesses to untold ages, stood motionless, their leaves trembling on the breath of a secret only they could hear. From the towering mountains to the lowliest valleys, nature itself was caught in the throes of an unseen awe.

It was as though time itself had been caught in an invisible web, each second suspended, neither moving forward nor backward but lingering in a moment pregnant with meaning. This was the paradox of the tomb's silence: to human eyes, the story seemed concluded, its pages closed in finality; yet beneath the surface, beyond the veil of mortal sight, a new chapter was already breathing into life, waiting to burst forth with the force of divine will.

The stars, those ancient firebrands crafted by the hand of God, had long witnessed mankind's fleeting histories, and now, they bore silent testament to the cosmic drama unfolding beneath their eternal watch. Each one, a blazing beacon in the night, flickered delicately as if in quiet anticipation, holding its sparks momentarily captive. Their light, suspended yet resolute, mirrored the very soul of creation: a deep yearning for redemption, for renewal, for the breaking of chains forged in shadow and sin.

Between these heavenly bodies, vast spaces of silence and mystery stretched on, reminding the world of the unfathomable depths of God's plan. What lay beyond the veil was not an ending, but a consummation, a transformation more profound than anything natural eyes could behold. The eternal light that the cosmos sought was about to pierce through the darkness of death itself, setting free a power impossible to contain or conquer.

Underneath the firmament, the earth held its breath, as though even the very ground sensed the coming miracle. The soil, rich with the bones of generations and the roots of creation, seemed to pulse with a silent heartbeat. It remembered the Garden, when man walked in communion with the Creator, and it ached for the restoration of broken fellowship. This longing, silent yet fierce, was as real as the winds that whispered through the branches.

Yet within the unseen realm, forces both divine and diabolical hovered at the precipice of action. The angels and archangels watched, poised to move at God's command, while the powers of darkness recoiled with loathing, sensing the impending unraveling of their dominion. The tension in the spiritual realm was palpable, a confrontation not just of power, but of eternal destiny. It was the climax of ages, the fulcrum upon which the fate of souls, and the very meaning of existence, would pivot.

This cosmic tension was captured not in noise or fury, but in the stillness, the silence pregnant with promise and dread, the weight of expectation pressing on the entire created order. The veil that separated heaven and earth, the seen and unseen, seemed thin and trembling, ready to be torn asunder. Such was the nature of the silence of the tomb, heavy not only with death but pregnant with the life to come.

The paradox of suspended time found its perfect expression here: though Jesus lay entombed, wrapped in the cold embrace of death, His divine nature writhed and prepared to break free. The crucible of Calvary was behind Him, His flesh weary and fallen, yet the Spirit that animated the universe was stirring within, gathering strength to burst forth in resurrection glory. This moment, the apparent end, contained the seeds of the greatest beginning the world had ever known.

Indeed, the very fabric of creation awaited the restoration that would flow from that empty tomb. The rivers, no longer silent, would ripple with new purpose. The winds would carry the song of victory. The stars would blaze anew with the fire of hope rekindled. And man, fallen yet beloved, would once again reach toward the Creator with the outstretched hands of grace and redemption.

For now, all was still. Suspended light hung in the night sky like an unfinished hymn, each note poised to soar but held momentarily in reverent restraint. Time itself seemed to fold inward, concentrating all creation's yearning into this single, divine fulcrum. The world was in waiting, silent, breathless, on the cusp of the miraculous.

This waiting was no passive state. It was an active, sacred holding, a divine patience that mirrored the heart of God, whose purposes were unshakable even in darkness. It called forth from humanity a stillness of soul, a surrender that recognized the limits of mortal understanding and the boundless depths of heavenly grace.

The silence of the tomb, and by extension, this silence of the world, served as a profound lesson. It showed that endings might camouflage beginnings, that apparent defeat hides ultimate victory. The mystery of divine time does not always conform to human expectation;

sometimes it demands that we trust in the hushed moments, in the spaces where light seems dim and hope faint, because that is where transformation stirs unseen.

Thus, the stage was set. The canvas of the universe awaited the brushstroke of resurrection. The curtain hung taut, ready to be drawn back and reveal a truth that would shake the very foundations of heaven and earth.

In this moment beyond moments, beyond words and eyes, the world, to all creation, was poised on the edge of a divine revelation. The silence was the breath before the song; the darkness the womb before the dawn; the pause the gathering of eternity's grace.

This is the silence of the tomb: not a silence of absence but of expectancy.

As the night deepened and the stars watched silently, the unseen realms shimmered with unspoken promise. The earth, holding its breath, awaited the dawn that would bring life to death, light to darkness, and hope to despair.

And in that waiting, the universe was being prepared for the inexhaustible power of the resurrection, the triumph of the Son of God over the grave, the shattering of the bonds of sin, and the opening of the gates of eternal life.

Within this sacred interval, suspended between worlds and moments, the heartbeat of redemption quickened. The cosmic drama of salvation, written in the heavens and etched into the soil of humanity, stood ready to unfold.

The world, ever watchful, ever hoping, waited.

Resurrection Dawn: Light Unbound

The Empty Tomb Discovered

The first rays of dawn spilled gently over the hills of Judea, painting the sky in hues of rose and gold. The silence of early morning was deep and still, broken only by the distant echo of birds beginning their day and the faint rustling of olive trees swaying in the cool breeze. The world seemed hushed, held in a sacred pause, as if nature itself anticipated the unfolding of a moment unlike any before. In that pristine light, the shadows that had clung tightly to the tomb where Jesus was laid began to waver and fade, surrendering to the inexorable touch of daybreak.

Upon this fragile cusp between night and morning, Mary Magdalene approached the sepulcher. Her steps were light but urgent, propelled by a trembling hope nested within a heart weighed by sorrow and confusion. The air was cool against her skin, and the familiar scent of earth and stone filled her nostrils, grounding her as she neared the entrance where the heavy stone had once barred the way. The cold, firm ground beneath her feet contrasted sharply with the warmth burning inside, a disquieting mix of grief and a faint, stubborn expectation brighter than any lamp.

She arrived at the tomb's mouth long before the sun had fully risen, the darkness still tangled in the angles of the carved rock face. The stone that sealed the grave, a massive slab, hewn and rolled by strong hands, was now mysteriously displaced. Her eyes caught the glimmer where the shadow had been breached, and a gasp rose silently from her chest. The barrier that had kept the body of Jesus within was no longer there. The stone was moved aside, as though the tomb itself had exhaled, releasing a secret kept too long.

Mary's breath came quicker, a flutter of heartbeats thrumming in sudden rhythm against the quiet morning. She reached out, her fingers brushing against the still coolness of the empty entrance, tracing the contours where the stone had rested. The cold stone was now smooth and undisturbed, yet hollow; a cavern of absence that spoke volumes louder than any presence.

Stepping inside, chilled air wrapped around her like a shroud, and the faint, damp scent of the tomb, earthy, raw, untouched by light, rolled through her senses. Everything was exactly as it had been prepared after the crucifixion, except that the body, the one she had come to mourn, was no longer there. Linen cloths, folded meticulously, lay in neat piles, a silent testimony to an event inexplicable and profound.

Her eyes darted from one corner to another, taking in every detail, the stone bench where the miserable body had been laid, the shadows clinging to the far wall, the silent emptiness that tasted of absence but hinted at hope. An icy tremor ran through her limbs, a mixture of disbelief and burgeoning wonder that stilled her very soul. How could this be? The man, bruised and broken, whom she had followed and loved, was not there.

The silence inside that tomb was unlike any silence she had ever known. It was not simply the absence of sound but a charged stillness that seemed to press against her ears and heart. It was the silence of a mystery revealed, a moment suspended between terror and triumph. Every fiber of her being was caught in a tension that pulled her deeper into a realm beyond mere human understanding.

Outside, the dawn grew brighter, and the first songs of morning birds sang a new melody. Light, soft and unyielding, poured into the dark chamber, illuminating the empty space with a radiance imbued not merely with physical brilliance but with something far more profound. It was the light of life, of resurrection, a dawn that did not flicker but blazed with the certainty of hope reborn.

Mary's thoughts raced. Was it a theft? Had someone come in the night to steal His body? Such questions swirled like a storm inside her heart, each answer giving way to another question that no words could answer. Yet, beneath it all lay a stirring, a whisper of a promise made and now fulfilled.

And then, in the gathering light, she remembered the words Jesus had spoken, words of resurrection and life. The scattered pieces of fear and doubt began to fit together like a divine tapestry woven in that very moment. The tomb was empty because He had risen, just as He said He would. This was no ordinary dawn; it was the dawning of eternity itself.

Her soul erupted into emotion, a strange blend of joy and fear, reverence and exultation. The very air seemed charged with a power invisible yet undeniable, as though creation held its breath and then exhaled in a symphony of praise. The earth beneath seemed to tremble softly, bearing witness to the truth that light had indeed conquered darkness and that death had been swallowed by life.

Mary's senses sharpened to every detail. The rough texture of the stone beneath her hand, the soft rustle of her garment in the cool breeze entering the tomb, the distant murmur of a world waking to something new. Her eyes filled with tears, yet they were tears of astonishment and awe, not of despair. Her lips trembled as she whispered His name, a sacred utterance that had the power to change everything.

In that hollow, empty chamber, the resurrection became more than a promise or a prophecy; it became a living reality. Every shadow and glimmer of dawn's light bore testimony to the victory over the grave. The silence was a sacred space, charged with the presence of the risen Christ, the source of hope and life for all who would believe.

Yet, even amid this dawning knowledge, Mary was caught in the delicate balance of disbelief. How could her eyes witness what her mind struggled to comprehend? The empty tomb, glowing with morning light, demanded faith in the unseen. It invited her to step beyond doubt and into the radiant mystery of resurrection life.

Her heart, once heavy with grief, now beat with a new rhythm, a cadence of hope that echoed through the silent valley. The cold stone of the tomb no longer held power over her; it was rendered meaningless by the presence of the risen Lord, whose very absence within that tomb proved the eternal truth.

As the sun climbed higher, painting the world with light and life, Mary Magdalene emerged from the tomb transformed. Not merely by sight or sound, but by a revelation so profound that it would ripple through the centuries and become the cornerstone of faith for countless souls.

Her footsteps, though hesitant, carried her outward to share the astonishing news, a message birthed in light and sealed by resurrection power. The empty tomb, once a symbol of death's finality, had become a beacon of unending hope, its silence now bursting with the promise of salvation and the dawn of a new covenant.

In the stillness of that moment, dawn and eternity met, and the world was forever changed. The resurrection was no longer distant or hidden; it stood revealed in the empty tomb, an everlasting testimony that life, in its fullest and most glorious form, had broken through the bonds of death and darkness.

Appearances and Affirmations

The early morning air was still crisp, and the first rays of dawn cast a gentle glow over the landscape as the reality of an empty tomb rippled through the hearts of Jesus' followers. The shadow of despair that had gripped them since the crucifixion began to wane, replaced slowly but surely by a dawning hope that defied the finality of death.

Into this fragile moment, God's greatest affirmation of all entered, the living Christ, risen and radiant, appearing among those who had walked with Him, teaching, comforting, and being known once again, forever altered by His unfathomable victory.

It was Mary Magdalene who first encountered the risen Lord on that morning, near the garden tomb where He had been laid. In her grief and confusion, she lingered weeping, unable to comprehend how the tomb could be empty and where her Master might have gone. In the silence, two angels spoke, their voices gentle messages of hope. And then Jesus Himself stood before her, His voice tender, calling her by name, "Mary." At once, recognition burst through her sorrow, and she reached out to Him with trembling hands. The grief that had held her captive transformed into overwhelming joy. The living presence of Jesus shattered the darkness. With a heart ablaze, Mary ran to share the good news, her voice alive with the sounds of hope.

Each subsequent appearance of Jesus carried with it a unique intimacy and power, weaving together the threads of recognition, teaching, and reassurance. In the closed room where fear and uncertainty had barred the doors, the disciples gathered in trembling silence. Suddenly, Jesus stood among them, greeting them with peace. The weight of their doubt was lifted as He showed them His hands and feet, wounds that bore testimony to the suffering He endured and the life He overcame. Thomas, who had needed to see and touch to believe, was invited to do so. His fingers traced the scars, his heart bursting with awe: "My Lord and my God!" From skepticism to worship, the encounter transformed fear into faith and despair into purpose.

Every visitation of Jesus was marked by a stark contrast to the grief left behind. The atmosphere shifted as light flooded in, both physically and spiritually. What had been shadows of death were replaced by brightness that spoke of eternal life. The senses were awakened anew, the softness of His voice, the weight of His touch, the sight of His scarred yet glorified body. These moments could not be contained by mere words; they were lived experiences that surpassed the boundaries of human expression. Laughter broke the criteria anew, filling spaces once consumed by tears; renewed friendship and boundless love radiated from Him, embracing broken hearts and restoring hope.

Jesus's conversation with His followers deepened their understanding of the divine purpose. He spoke of the Scriptures, prophecies fulfilled and promises made good. The reality of His death and resurrection was no mere miracle; it was the fulfillment of God's plan for redemption. As the disciples listened, their hearts burned with eagerness and awe, and their fear turned into boldness. Each word was an affirmation that the life laid down had been restored, more than restored, transformed into eternal life that death could not hold.

On the shores of the Sea of Galilee, the risen Jesus revealed Himself again to seven disciples as they toiled in the early morning. After a fruitless night of fishing, He called out to them to cast their net once more. The catch was miraculous, bursting with abundance just as their faith once again surged in the presence of the risen Christ. A simple yet profound meal followed, the bread and fish shared as a sacred fellowship that transcended tragedy. There, Jesus reinstated Peter, tenderly restoring him after his denial, entrusting him with the care of His flock. The affirmation was not only of His resurrection but also of the continued mission, love, shepherdship, and witness.

These appearances serve as bridges between the realms of mortal sorrow and divine joy. Each moment illuminated the truth that death was not the final word and that God's presence remained unbroken. The disciples, once scattered in fear, became emboldened apostles, their hearts ignited by encounters with the risen Lord. They bore witness not only to a spiritual truth but to a tangible reality that transformed their lives and the course of history.

The narrative of Jesus's post-resurrection visits carries with it a profound theological significance. It reveals the nature of the resurrection as both a personal and communal event, where the living Christ remains present among His people. Through recognition, whether by sight, voice, or touch, Jesus bridges the divide between the mortal and the eternal, affirming that life is victorious and God's love is unending. These moments are not frozen in time but continue to speak to believers, inviting them into the same transformative experience of hope, restoration, and mission.

Each scene pulsates with a new creation's vitality. Where tears once flowed, laughter now rings out. Where silence had reigned, joyous testimony bursts forth. The disciples' journey from disbelief to conviction mirrors the spiritual journey of every believer, inviting us to witness the power that ushers in life from death. In Jesus's appearances, the transcendent brightness of resurrection dawn breaks through all shadows, and the soul recognizes the presence of the eternal Light that cannot be extinguished.

These divine visitations culminate in the great commissioning given on a mountain in Galilee, where Jesus's presence radiates not only peace but authority. He commissions His followers to go forth and make disciples of all nations, baptizing them and teaching them to observe all that He commanded. This final affirmation is a call to participate in the ongoing story of redemption, energized by the very power of the resurrection itself.

As the apostles and disciples prepare to witness the ascension, their hearts are full, not of fear or uncertainty, but of joy and expectation. They have seen with their own eyes, heard with their own ears, and touched with their own hands the living Christ. This tangible proof of the resurrection transforms their entire being and sets in motion the unstoppable advance of the Gospel.

In the radiant light of these moments, death's hold is forever broken, and new life is undeniable. The appearances and affirmations of Jesus after His resurrection are the cornerstone of Christian faith, testifying that Jesus is alive, that God's promises endure, and that His divine presence walks still with His people. Through these sacred encounters, the dawn of resurrection becomes a perpetual light, unbound, unfading, and full of hope.

The Promise of Eternal Light

As the radiant dawn follows the long, dark night, so too does the resurrection of Jesus Christ illuminate the vast expanse of human existence with a light that is both unquenchable and eternal. This light, born from the heart of God and manifested in the empty tomb, stands as the supreme promise of hope, the embodiment of divine love that neither death, despair, nor darkness can ever extinguish. In this holy triumph, the eternal dawn breaks forth, heralding not only the victory of the Son over the grave but also the unfathomable depth of God's grace extended to all who believe.

We stand at the threshold of what the apostle John describes with awe: "That was the true Light, which lighteth every man that cometh into the world" (John 1:9). This Light, manifest in the incarnate Word, shone brightest when Jesus rose from the dead, casting away the shadows that had long enveloped creation since the fall. The resurrection is thus far more than an event recorded in ancient scrolls; it is the perpetual beacon guiding the lost, the weary, and the broken toward the peace and joy found only in the presence of the risen Christ. It proclaims a transformation profound enough to rewrite the destiny of humanity itself.

This promise of eternal light is rooted deeply in Scripture, resonating through the testimonies of Jesus' followers and the inspired words of the prophets. Isaiah, centuries before the coming of the

Messiah, had proclaimed, "Arise, shine; for thy light is come, and the glory of the LORD is risen upon thee" (Isaiah 60:1). These words find their ultimate fulfillment on the resurrection morning, when the glory of the Lord, embodied in Jesus Christ's conquered grave, enveloped the earth in a brilliance that can never fade. The darkness that once claimed dominion over death was broken, and in its place, the dawn of eternal life rose, unrelenting and radiant.

The apostle Paul, penning letters under the inspiration of the Holy Spirit, captures this profound reality when he writes: "For if we believe that Jesus died and rose again, even so them also which sleep in Jesus will God bring with him" (1 Thessalonians 4:14). Here, resurrection becomes not just a historical fact but a living hope, a cornerstone of Christian faith that assures believers of their own eventual victory over death. It is a hope that reaches beyond mortal limitation, proclaiming the promise of transformation, renewal, and perpetuity in the presence of God. The resurrection light is neither flicker nor spark; it is an eternal flame kindled by divine glory.

To meditate on the resurrection as a beacon of hope is to grasp the immense theological significance it bears. It reveals a God who, in His infinite love, did not abandon humankind to the fate of sin and death but reached into the abyss with saving hands, raising a new creation out of the ruins. The resurrection testifies to the power of God's love, a love that is more powerful than the grave and more enduring than the darkest night. It is the ultimate victory cry ringing through the corridors of time: "Death is swallowed up in victory" (1 Corinthians 15:54). This triumphant proclamation ignites an unwavering hope within the heart of every believer.

Yet, beyond cosmic victory, the resurrection light carries a deeply personal and transformative power. It bids each individual to leave behind the shadows of despair, guilt, and fear, and to step into a reality illuminated by grace and mercy. The resurrection invites a renewed vision of faith, not merely as a doctrinal statement but as a living experience of transformation. It beckons souls to arise from the tombs of brokenness and sin, to embrace the possibility of new life enlivened by the presence of Christ. In this new light, believers find the courage to confront struggles with steadfastness, the strength to forgive, and the peace to love unconditionally.

John's gospel captures this transformative power with poetic clarity: "I am the light of the world: he that followeth me shall not walk in darkness, but shall have the light of life" (John 8:12). This declaration is neither abstract nor symbolic alone; it is an invitation into a vibrant and ongoing relationship with the risen Savior. To walk in the light of life is to live in the unfolding reality of resurrection power, to experience daily renewal as new creations in Christ (2 Corinthians 5:17). The glory of the resurrection thus spills into every aspect of existence, a constant dawn dispelling night, a continuous spring nourishing the thirsty soul.

In this light, the Christian journey becomes one of continual awakening, a perpetual resurrection from the death of sin to the life of righteousness. The promise of eternal light fuels perseverance amid trials and encourages believers to embody the hope they profess. The resurrection is not merely the culminating chapter of Jesus' earthly ministry; it is the genesis of a divine movement that transforms the world through the power of love made manifest. This movement is infused with a radiant joy that refuses to be dimmed, a peace that transcends understanding, and a love that conquers fear.

Moreover, the resurrection light carries profound communal dimensions. As the early church gathered in the shadow of the empty tomb, they were filled with a hope that shaped their lives and their witness: "And they continued stedfastly in the apostles' doctrine and fellowship, and in breaking of bread, and in prayers" (Acts 2:42). The resurrection cultivates a community marked by love, unity, and a shared mission to spread this light to all corners of the earth. It is a light that knows no boundaries, racial, cultural, or socioeconomic, and it calls believers to be agents of reconciliation and peace, bearing witness to the power of Christ's triumph.

This radiant hope also challenges the believer to live as a visible manifestation of the resurrection light amidst a world often overshadowed by despair and darkness. To carry the light of Christ means to confront injustice with courage, to comfort the suffering with compassion, and to proclaim the good news with boldness. It means living a life that glows with the fruit of the Spirit, love, joy, peace, longsuffering, gentleness, goodness, faith (Galatians 5:22–23), so that others, drawn by this illumination, might be led to the source of all hope, Jesus Christ Himself.

The apostle Peter captures the urgency and privilege of this calling when he exhorts believers to be "a chosen generation, a royal priesthood, a holy nation, a peculiar people; that ye should shew forth the praises of him who hath called you out of darkness into his marvelous light: Which in time past were not a people, but are now the people of God" (1 Peter 2:9–10). The promise of eternal light is not a private treasure to be hidden but a dazzling reality to be shared, a beacon leading others from the gloom of sin to the brilliance of salvation.

And so, the meditation on resurrection dawn unfolds into a life-wide commitment, a response to the unbound light that calls believers onward. It invites a surrender to the transforming power of grace, an openness to be shaped by the Spirit, and a boldness to proclaim the life that overcomes death. This light shines not only in moments of ecstatic joy but also in trials, suffering, and sacrifice, affirming that Christ's victory is deep and unshakable even in the darkest valleys.

To embrace the resurrection as the promise of eternal light is also to enter into the eschatological hope, the confident expectation of the new heaven and new earth where God shall wipe away all tears (Revelation 21:4). It is a hope that looks beyond the present to the glorious consummation of all things, where the effects of sin, pain, and death are forever abolished. The resurrection is the first fruits of this coming reality, the pledge that nothing can thwart the divine plan of restoration and redemption. In this forward-looking hope, believers find assurance and inspiration to press on faithfully.

In reflecting on this, the psalmist's words echo with fresh power: "Thy word is a lamp unto my feet, and a light unto my path" (Psalm 119:105). The resurrection is the divine lamp shining in the darkness of a fallen world, guiding feet that stumble, illuminating paths that seem uncertain. It is a light that clarifies God's promises, affirms His faithfulness, and strengthens the heart against fear. Carrying this light within, believers become reflections of God's glory, conduits of His peace and love.

This teaching draws us back to the very heart of the gospel, the glorious mystery of God's incarnation, sufferings, death, and resurrection accomplished for the salvation of humanity. The eternal light that bursts forth on resurrection dawn is the ultimate expression of divine love and power. It proclaims that no force can extinguish the grace freely given to all who receive it by faith. It invites all to partake in the divine life inaugurated on that first Easter morning, a life unbounded by time and shadowed only by the horizon of God's infinite presence.

As readers meditate on the life and resurrection of Jesus Christ, they are invited into a place of quiet awe and overwhelming gratitude, a place where spiritual vision is rekindled and hope is reborn. The empty tomb speaks not just of death defeated but of life eternal secured; it calls out to every soul in need of healing and renewal to embrace the light now shining forth in the world.

Thus, the promise of eternal light is not a distant, abstract truth but a vibrant, living reality, one that ignites faith, fosters transformation, and anchors the believer in the unchanging love of God. It is a dawn without end, a flame that never ceases to burn, a love eternal that beckons all to come and see, to believe, and to walk in the everlasting light of Christ.

May this profound truth stir within each heart a renewed commitment to live as children of the resurrection, bearers of the divine light, and heralds of the dawn unbounded. In the power of His rising, may all find hope unshakable, faith renewed, and love eternal, so that the world may be drawn ever closer to the heart of God, where light reigns forevermore.

Thank You, Bold Explorer!

We've reached the final stop on this wild ride, and what a ride it has been! I hope these pages have sparked your curiosity, challenged your thinking, and filled your world with fresh ideas. Your choice to dive into this book means you're one of the bold thinkers ready to explore beyond the ordinary.

This journey was crafted not just to inform, but to ignite passion and inspire change. Whether you found answers, new questions, or simply a fresh perspective, know that your engagement breathes life into every word written here. It's your enthusiasm that transforms these pages into a living dialogue.

I want to say a huge thank you for investing your time and attention. You made the words meaningful by reading them, by allowing yourself to be part of this story. Your presence matters, and it fuels the fire that keeps books like this alive and relevant.

Remember, the end of a book is just the beginning of new thoughts, new discussions, and new adventures. Take what you've learned here and let it ripple through your world, share it, question it, and build upon it.

Until next time, keep that spark alive, keep challenging the status quo, and never stop exploring the extraordinary. The world is bigger, deeper, and more fascinating than we can imagine. So go out and make your own stories worthy of the pages you've just turned.

Stay curious, stay fearless, and most importantly, stay YOU.

With endless gratitude and unstoppable energy!

Gary E. Risenhoover